WITNESS TO THE HELLFIRE OF GENOCIDE

A Testimony from Gaza

Wasim Said

Published in October 2025 by
1804 Books, New York, NY

1804Books.com

This selection © 1804 Books, New York, NY
ISBN: 979-8-9990195-1-6
Library of Congress Control Number: 2025944772

Translation by Dr. Muhammad Tutunji, edited by 1804 Books, Liberated Texts,
and the People's Center for Palestine

Cover by Vivek Venkatraman
Map by Gareth BF
Photos by Wasim Said
Cover photo by Ali Hamad

"Wasim Said describes what life in Gaza has become since October 9 with a sorrowful pen, showing that for Palestinians, even eating is an act of resistance. The pages of this book are filled with tales of famine, killings and losses. But, there is something that the 'monsters' cannot erase: the love among families and the love for the land."

— *Francesca Albanese*
UN Special Rapporteur on the Occupied Palestinian Territories

"*Witness to the Hellfire* is an urgent collection of writing that challenges the limitations of passive witness and the limitations of prioritizing feeling over action. When Said writes 'I did not write this to make you cry,' in the intro, it is a charge for the reader to place real intent in how they spend time with the language that comes after. Language of survival and deep affection for a place and people under siege, and under the brutalities of an ongoing occupation. Wherever this book meets you, the writing within it, of lost friends and family members and memories, should live alongside you in a way that moves you towards urgent action. This work is a living history, which will endure for years to come, just as Palestine and its people will endure for years to come."

— *Hanif Aburraqib*
author of They Can't Kill Us Until They Kill Us

"All future generations to come will speak about a people of immense courage who, under the hardest circumstances, still found the way to document the horrors of genocide and ethnic cleansing. They will speak about people like Wasim who, with talent and commitment, educated so many about eight decades of Zionist violations and the hypocrisy of nations that claimed to be the representatives of human rights and democracy but were actually complicit in a system that exploits, oppresses, and destroys life all around the world. Millions now understand what Zionism, imperialism, and colonialism are, and they will never stop mobilizing against these great evils of our generation. That's why this book is not only important for its words, but because it's a testimony of a period of great violations that, in the end, planted the seeds of a new world inspired by Palestinians like Wasim and his people's *sumud*."

— *Thiago Ávila*
Freedom Flotilla

Dedication

To the souls of the martyrs,

who have never faded from memory,

nor dimmed in our hearts.

And to those with undaunted consciences,

who remember that behind every number lies a human being—

and a story that deserves to be told.

Table of Contents

Foreword

Exactly ten years before his martyrdom by an Israeli airstrike—alongside his brother, sister, and their children: Alaa, Yahya, and Mohammad—Palestinian writer and academic Dr. Refaat Alareer wrote the following in the introduction to the book *Gaza Writes Back*: "The more savage Israel becomes, the stronger the reasons Gazans find to cling to life and to remain steadfast on their land." Dr. Refaat continued, "Many in Gaza have sworn to fight in its defense; many others have sworn to protect the fighters' backs. Some Gazans turned to their pens or keyboards, swearing to expose Israel's aggression through writing."

No one could have imagined the depth and extent of Gaza's commitment to that vow—or how enduring the bond would be between escalating brutality and the will to resist it by every means possible, first and foremost through writing.

According to Israel's logic, "What cannot be achieved through force, will be achieved through more force." But what brutality remains to be unleashed on a people beyond genocide itself?

Yes, we must be cautious not to romanticize resilience—to avoid masking the scale of the tragedy, injustice, betrayal, and complicity by exporting the image of the invincible Gazan hero, as though they are anything less than human. Too often, we indulge in the fantasy of heroism as a way to ease the shame of our failure to stand with them.

Forgetting that before they are heroes, they are oppressed—utterly isolated, in a loneliness unlike any before. That is why before we weave our relationship with the hero, we must weave it with the oppressed. The former offers a false comfort; the latter demands action, discomfort, and a call for commitment to fight for justice. These two Hero/Oppressed definitions do not cancel each other out—but we must understand: these heroes are, first and foremost, oppressed. "The wretched of the earth," in Franz Fanon's terms.

Exactly one hundred years ago, Zionist theorist Vladimir Jabotinsky wrote his infamous article "The Iron Wall," declaring that "[Arab people] make such enormous concessions on such fateful questions only when there is no hope left. Only when not a single breach is visible in the iron wall," Yet, this book stands as hope itself. It is one of those cracks.

Written by an oppressed hero under such extraordinary circumstances, this book proves that Jabotinsky, and every Zionist theorist after him, were wrong. And it reaffirms, once again, that Dr. Refaat Alareer was right, as it offers a living answer to the vow Dr. Refaat spoke of.

Genocide embodies the most intense form of concentrated death and mass killing against the human race. While the literature on genocide often emerges after the fact—through survivors' testimonies—this text documents it *as it happens*. Zionist warplanes soar above it, their drones hum nearby, while the pen and paper seek refuge beneath the cloth of a displacement tent, writing in the shadow of hunger and famine.

The writer did not retrieve these moments from distant memory; he lived them, moment by moment, as he wrote them. This was not writing *about* death, but writing *within* it, surrounded by it. And this is what the reader must first understand: every scene recorded here, every scream, every shelling, was not merely a subject to be written about—it was a living reality invading the act of writing itself. The very process of documentation cried out for its own documentation. This foreword is merely a humble attempt to cast light on that.

So when you read, do not overlook the sound of warplanes, the explosions, the sirens—they still pierce through every line and slip between the words, because they are, quite simply, part of the text itself.

In late April, my friend Louis Allday sent me the first draft of the manuscript, along with a note: *"You must read this—and we have a duty to help publish it."* That was the beginning of my communication with Wasim. In the very first voice note he sent me, Wasim shared his reasons for writing this testimony. His motivation reflects the inner thinking of a person besieged by an unbearable magnitude of death—its multiplicities, its fractures.

He spoke of resisting the collective erasure of families—of entire lineages being slaughtered. He refused to let them vanish into oblivion. Someone had to give them meaning, to preserve their memory. And that is what Wasim took upon himself.

But Wasim didn't write *after* surviving. He wrote from within that narrow corridor of life amid the crush of massacres. And in every message and recording between us, he repeated: *"My aim is to leave a mark"* and *"not to be forgotten."* This text is his personal answer to a question that haunted every Gazan: *Will I die and be forgotten? Will my death pass as though I never was?* Or as one person bitterly put it: "If I'm lucky enough to be martyred, to be wrapped in a shroud, to have a funeral—I'll be remembered for two hours, then it's over. As if I never existed."

Wasim wrote to break that forgetting—to give those who left a trace, and those who remained a sense of solace: that someone had witnessed, had recorded, amidst death, that they were here.

And here, precisely, lies Wasim's courage. In this act, he may have embodied the very courage of Gaza. A young man in his early twenties, rebelling against an imposed end, refusing to be erased in silence. In a moment that might be the most harrowing in human history—a death that's wide-scale, technologically advanced, and globally enabled—Wasim wrote, with nothing but paper and pen.

He spoke to me at length about his moments of doubt, moments when he questioned the meaning of it all. He nearly surrendered to despair, almost stopping many times. But he carried on. For Wasim, writing wasn't just expression; it was the physical act of answering the most philosophical of questions: *What does it mean to live?* For him, meaning wasn't abstract—it was action: *If I do not write, it is as if I never lived.*

And because he is Gazan, Wasim's answer was never an individual escape, never selfish—it was collective. In the text, you see him hesitate, embarrassed even to speak about himself, and he asks: *What about my community? What about those who never got the chance to write?* Soon, the text becomes theirs. He wrote on their behalf in one of the noblest forms of self-sacrifice, following the steps of his brothers and sisters of the Palestinians *fedayeens*, or resitance fighters. Wasim did not carry a weapon. He stood, with his pen, in their place.

This collective spirit flows through the text, just as it flows through Gaza in the solidarity of people under genocide. Genocide, as a concept, is not merely mass killing. It is a systematic colonial process aiming to dismantle the colonized society, its material structures, institutions, and self-organization. But at its deepest level, it aims to destroy the *moral* structure of that society, to fracture it into scattered individuals, each preying on the other to survive.

And here arises this testimony—not only as a daily record of generosity, selflessness, truth, and cooperation, but as proof, in itself, of an astonishing resilience in the moral structure of this community under genocide. This, precisely, is what anthropology must learn from Gaza: that despite the magnitude of the genocide, despite Zionism's belief that its policies would produce a society the reflects its own monstrous image, the moral fabric of Gazan society has remained remarkably intact, even as long as the genocide has continued.

This does not mean it went unshaken. Yes, a segment of exploitative traders emerged. Organized crime harmed people just as the occupation did, and Wasim speaks painfully of his encounters with them. But total collapse? That never happened.

This society held onto its image of itself—its Palestinian and Arab identity, its moral and cultural system. A significant part of it refused to let go, as if echoing Wasim's search for the meaning of life, but at the scale of an entire people, the Palestinian people.

The enormous toll of death left its mark on Wasim. Everything became urgent, rushed, as if life itself were narrowing fast. He was literally running, Zionist death chasing behind. He pleaded with us to hasten the book's publication—unsure whether he would live to see it. I would ask him what he had to eat while writing, in the height of famine. He would reply: a disk of bread made from ground lentils, or a bit of rice.

Still, Wasim endured. He wrote, not only to survive, but to awaken a duty within us.

This testimony, with its clarity, logic, and living embodiment of the intellectual's role—and of culture's power as long theorized by philosophy—is not merely a document. It is a message from the deepest depths of the valley of death, from the hellfire of genocide, to the Arabs and to all of humanity. A message that says: death, even on this scale, did not strip Wasim—and did not strip Gaza—of their value system. They did not relinquish dignity, courage, effort, solidarity, pride, nationalism, or resistance.

And so each of us is faced with the great moral and national question: we, from within our lives of comfort and consumption—what is *our* excuse?

— *Mousa Alsadah*

Preface

In the spring of 2024, a collective effort began on social media to share fundraisers for displaced people in Gaza and assist them in whatever other ways possible. By a quirk of fate, the first few people that I helped in this way were all from Beit Hanoun. As they began to ask me to help family members and friends of theirs in turn, I ended up forming a connection with an extended network of families, friends, and neighbors, all of whom were from that small, now-demolished city in the northeast of Gaza. Wasim, the author of this book, is one of that group.

From our early interactions in September 2024, Wasim's fierce intelligence shone through, as did his curiosity and desire to learn. These are undoubtedly admirable traits in any circumstances, but they were and remain utterly remarkable when considering the dire situation that Wasim faced and still faces. He desperately wanted to continue his formal education in physics, and at the same time began to ask me for things to read, while also seeking my opinion on global issues ("Is China socialist?," "What's your stance on Syria?" and so on). It quickly became clear to me that Wasim was not a typical young man in his early twenties.

When the ceasefire was agreed in January 2025, Wasim, like so many others from Beit Hanoun, immediately returned north to his hometown from his enforced displacement in the south. I remember being moved by the excitement and near-joy that Wasim and many others expressed to me about being able to return home, even in the knowledge that most of their houses and much else in the city, including the seven-hundred-year-old Umm al-Nasr mosque, had been destroyed by Zionist forces. They defiantly returned to their land regardless and got to work tidying up and stabilizing their bombed-out homes to the best of their abilities, clearing the streets of debris, and, in some cases, planting fruit trees in the hope of receiving a harvest later in the year. Their unbreakable connection to that small corner of Gaza, of Palestine, was humbling, tangible, and full of love. It was during that moment of relative respite that Wasim began to write about what he had experienced from October 2023 up to that point. Before long, as they do habitually, the Zionists broke the ceasefire, and so the displacement and mass killing started all over again, shattering the fragile sense of cautious optimism I had seen emerging in Wasim and others around him.

Wasim's account is harrowing. The first time I read it in full I felt devastated and enraged anew, despite already being familiar with elements of the narrative. Wasim conveys the horror, misery, and fear of the genocide in a way that few other accounts I have read do, yet crucially he also captures a sense of the solidarity, community, faith, and love that persist regardless.

The act of resistance, John Berger once wrote, "is not only refusing to accept the absurdity of the world-picture offered us, but denouncing it. And when hell is denounced from within, it ceases to be hell."[1] These words immediately came to my mind when, sometime in March 2025, Wasim first asked me whether I thought it was a good idea for him to write a book about his experiences of the genocide. My answer was an immediate and resounding yes, and now, as I contemplate the result of Wasim's

---

1   John Berger, "Against the great defeat of the world," *Race & Class*, 40/2–3, 1999.

efforts, Berger's sentiment informs how I believe this remarkable document must be treated. Wasim's text is not simply a moving and gut-wrenching testimony of genocide and displacement, but rather a defiant act of resistance to it, written, as Mousa Alsadah notes in this book's foreword, not in retrospect from a position of safety as is typical of this genre, but from within an ongoing nightmare—from within hell itself. It constitutes a powerful example of what Ghassan Kanafani termed "resistance litera-ture," and as the martyr Kanafani himself argued, the "extreme importance of the cultural form of resistance is no less valuable than armed resistance itself."[2]

The martyr Refaat Alareer also understood this central role of literature. In a 2019 lecture about the poet Fadwa Tuqan and the importance of cultural resistance, Alareer stated:

> Of course, we always fall into this trap of saying, "She [Fadwa Tuqan] was arrested for just writing poetry!" We do this a lot, even us believers in litera-ture . . . [we say], "Why would Israel arrest somebody or put someone under house arrest? She only wrote a poem?" So, we contradict ourselves sometimes; we believe in the power of literature changing lives as a means of resistance, as a means of fighting back, and then at the end of the day, we say, "She just wrote a poem!" We shouldn't be saying that.

The Palestinians' enemies have long understood the power and significance of cultural resistance of this kind. When Israeli forces invaded Beirut in 1982, one of their first targets was the Pal-estine Liberation Organization's (PLO) Palestine Research Center, the library and archive of which were looted wholesale. This attack was part of a broader Israeli onslaught in which its occupation forces "wiped out most of the Palestinian educational and cultural

---

2   Ghassan Kanafani, quoted in Barbara Harlow, *Resistance Literature* (1987), 11.

institutions [in Lebanon that] they could get their hands on."[3]
When asked about this destruction not long after Israel's with-
drawal, the Palestinian poet Mahmoud Darwish gave an answer
that is worth quoting at length:

> The condition for Israeli existence is the recognition
> by the external world of its civilizational superiority
> over land that it claims was without people. And if
> this process is based on an assault against culturally
> unproductive people, then in the Western concep-
> tion it is regarded as a civilizing mission. The devel-
> opment of Palestinian cultural activity compelled
> Israel to eradicate anything that has to do with a past
> relation, a present relation, or a future testimony.
> Consequently, I was not surprised by the Israeli
> destruction of cultural institutions, for it is a part of
> the Israeli destruction of the Palestinian homeland,
> Palestinian society, and Palestinian testimony before
> history, because he who steals land does not surprise
> us by stealing a library. [4]

I thought of Darwish's words more than once while reading
Wasim's account, for it is in this context that the devastation,
killing, and cruelty that he so vividly depicts—and is still living
through—must be understood. What has been unleashed upon
Gaza is a calculated campaign of destruction—an inescapable
part of Zionism's all-encompassing war against Palestinian existence, identity, and memory. It is for this reason that Wasim's
testimony must be considered an act of resistance in itself, a
defiant manifestation of his refusal to be silenced and forgotten in the face of a cruel, sadistic enemy devoid of any shred of
humanity. Wasim's desire to record the stories and memories of

---

3   Munir Fasheh, "Graham-Brown, Education, Repression and Liberation,"
     MERIP, 136/137, October–December 1985.
4   With thanks to Robert K. Beshara for transcribing and translating this extract
     taken from the film *Palestinian Identity* (dir. Kassem Hawal, 1984).

those around him, both living and dead, is a moving reflection of the collective commitment of the Palestinian people to one another and to their land, a commitment that is ongoing amidst a genocide of unimaginable depravity and scale.

The emotional impact of reading Wasim's words will vary reader by reader. My own reaction was multifaceted, but above all I felt (and still feel) an overwhelming sense of obligation to fight for the sake of Wasim and every single person in Gaza in whatever way I can. As Wasim himself tells us in his own introduction: "I need a reader who won't just close the book and sigh, then go to sip their coffee."

This mention of coffee immediately reminded me of a speech that George Habash gave fifty-five years ago, when shortly before their safe release he addressed a group of Western hostages the PFLP had briefly held in an Amman hotel, and attempted to explain his way of thinking to them:

> People living in different circumstances think on different lines . . . [w]e don't wake up in the morning to have a cup of milk with Nescafe and then spend half an hour in front of the mirror thinking of flying to Switzerland or having one month in this country or one month in that country . . . we, the Palestinian people, and the conditions we have been living in . . . have modeled our way of thinking. We cannot help it. You can understand our way of thinking when you know a very basic fact. We, the Palestinians . . . for the last twenty-two years, have been living in camps and tents. We were driven out of our country . . . driven out like sheep and left here in refugee camps in very inhumane conditions.[5]

---

5   George Habash, "Our Code of Morals is Our Revolution," 1970.

It is now seventy-seven years since the Nakba, and the Palestinians (and those in Gaza most of all) remain in inhumane conditions. The Nakba has not ended, and as such this book must not be treated as simply a lamentation of tragedies past, for it is a rallying cry from within a bloody struggle of the highest possible stakes. We must heed its call to action. We must not content ourselves with expressions of mourning for what has already happened, but instead commit ourselves to try to change what has yet to unfold in whatever way our circumstances allow.

To the martyrs of Gaza and all those who love them.

— Louis Allday
Liberated Texts
July 2025

Note from the People's Center for Palestine and 1804 Books

Written amidst the urgency of documenting everything, in the effort to preserve all that continues to be stolen, *Witness to the Hellfire of Genocide* follows the tradition of Palestinian testimony, a genre born from three generations of Palestinian intellectuals and artists that record the ongoing Nakba. Stories in this tradition share universal features: honoring the martyrs of the Palestinian cause; documenting the war crimes erased by Zionist and imperialist sources; and capturing the collective spirit, resistance, and dignity of the Palestinian people. As the author, Wasim Said, reflects in the aftermath of his first displacement from his home in Beit Hanoun: "My people are great and generous despite everything they endure."

What distinguishes this text from the others that have come before it, is that Wasim wrote it during the genocide on Gaza, not after. As the two-year anniversary of the genocide approached, as the massacres, the torture in Zionist detention camps, starvation, and systemic destruction of all of Gaza's social infrastructure continued and intensified, it only became more urgent to publish this text. In many ways, it is an impossible challenge to truly capture the depth of truth and feeling that Wasim conveys in each of his stories, because the horrors he encounters are unspeakable. During this unprecedented moment in the history of the Palestinian struggle, the group which came together to translate Wasim's writing experienced its gravity, urgency, and significance—but not in a way that was limited to the pages. For each of us, it was clear that this book is a painful gift which holds its readers, including ourselves, to account for our commitment and attention towards Gaza every day the genocide continues, and everyday towards Palestine until liberation and return.

We are commonly told to study our history in order to best act in the present. But Wasim's testimony comes from a genocide happening right now, in our present. It is a call to transform our history now, not after the fact, years or even generations later. It is a call to be participants and subjects of our histories, transforming the unjust world we live in today. Wasim explains, this is why he decided to document how his loved ones were killed and his people were exterminated: "I write . . . so I can hang these words around your neck—to make you bear the responsibility of my perspective, the responsibility of knowing, the responsibility of being a witness."

Throughout his account, Wasim directly addresses the reader. In these moments, he is very clear: his words are not an invitation for sorrow. We—those of us who open this book's pages—are not supposed to read, despair, and then move on with our days and lives. Wasim's testimony will undoubtedly lead readers to shed tears and there is no shame in that; there is shame, however, in witnessing without action. Ultimately, this book is an instrument for intervening against the genocide. It is a living documentation of a brutal extermination process that is being actively denied and whitewashed, and those who dare to expose the horrors of Zionist occupation are targeted and attacked. This book is a call to commit to the humanity of the struggle for Palestinian liberation, and it demands us to move and to make the world move for Gaza.

Scenes from the author's tent where he wrote

Witness to the Hellfire of Genocide:
A Testimony from Gaza

Introduction

I didn't plan to write this book like this.
And no—I didn't start writing under the bombs,
    as you might think.

I began after the war paused.
After the ceasefire in January 2025, when we returned to
    Beit Hanoun—what was left of it.
The town was rubble. But we were breathing life again.

I came back with one thought:
To write what I lived through.
To end with hope—with return, with dust, with air, with
    home—even if the home was just ruins.

I imagined the ending would be like dawn after a long night.
That moment of walking into our street,
Breathing in the smell of Beit Hanoun,
Welcoming its people like a mother welcomes a child
    who almost drowned.

But

the moment I picked up the pen—
The war returned.

I didn't finish the first chapter
Before we were displaced again.
This time it was worse.
More violent.
More painful.

I wrote from my tent.
Or rather, from my despair.
I write as I gasp for breath between the shells;
I write, and each word might be the last.

The sound of planes hasn't stopped.
My younger siblings cry from hunger and fear.
And all I have are these pages.

I didn't write this to make you cry.
Not for you to tell me: *"Poor you."*
I write it so I can hang these words around your neck—
to make you bear the responsibility of my perspective,
the responsibility of knowing,
the responsibility of being a witness.

This isn't mere literature.
It's a testimony under fire.
A voice in a time when truth is no longer
    to be found on screens.
A testimony from a wound that refuses to heal,
    so its voice may remain alive.

I don't need your sympathy.
I need a conscience that hasn't rotted.
A human who hasn't turned to stone.

I need a reader who won't just close the book and sigh,
Then go to sip their coffee.

I wrote so the massacre won't be forgotten.
So my name remains.
So my town's name remains.
So the faces of my siblings remain—
The ones who lived through genocide searching
    for burnt bread,
Or a mattress torn by shrapnel.

Read this not as a novel.
But as you would read a gravestone.
As if a voice from beneath the ground was saying:

"I was here. And I could have lived—
If only you had said something."

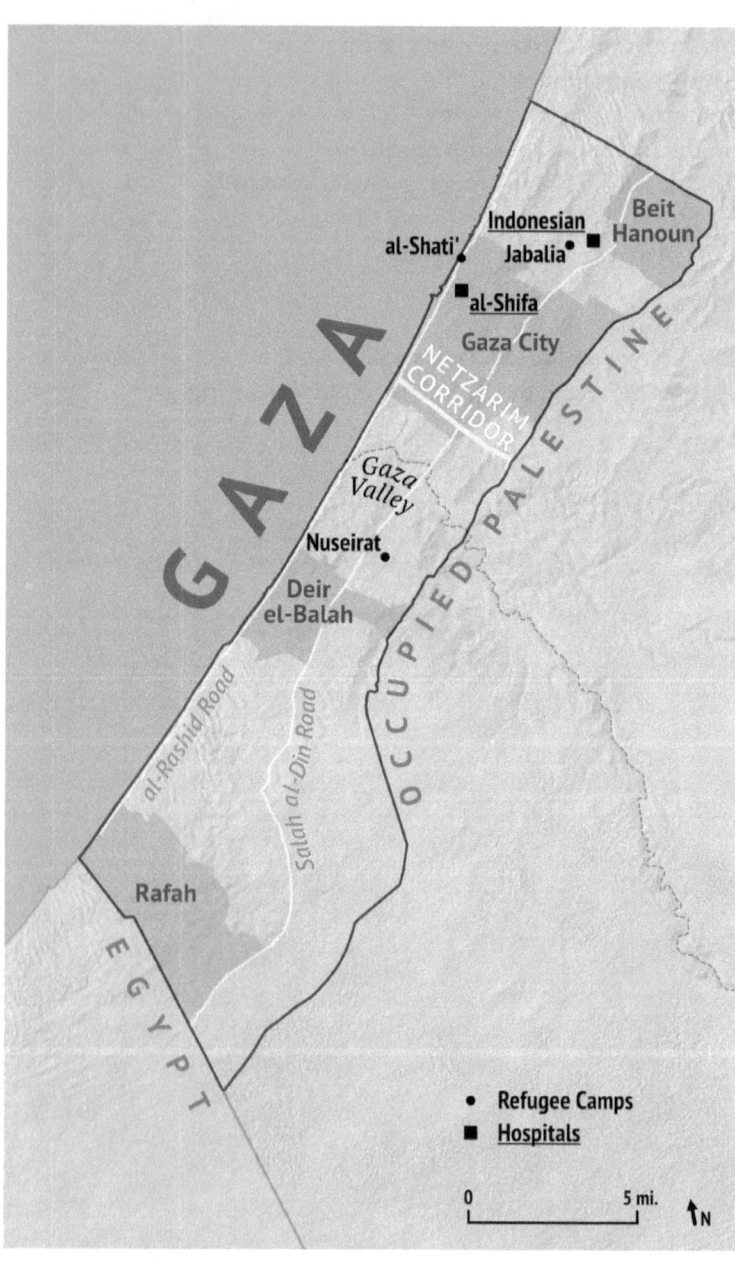

GAZA

OCCUPIED PALESTINE

EGYPT

Indonesian
al-Shati' • Jabalia ■
Beit
Hanoun

■ al-Shifa

Gaza City

NETZARIM
CORRIDOR

Gaza
Valley

Nuseirat •

Deir
el-Balah

al-Rashid Road

Salah al-Din Road

Rafah

• Refugee Camps
■ Hospitals

0   5 mi.

↑N

My Journey from Home to Tent

On the evening of October 7, death began to crawl towards Beit Hanoun, an army of human locusts devouring anything in its path, an endless barrage of shells turning everything into rubble.

My family gathered on the ground floor of our building, all thirty-six of us, my grandfather and everyone bearing his name. We sat in complete silence with the burning questions in our minds:

Where can we go?

What will happen to us?!

Our hearts were racing. The sound of explosions refused to be silenced.

In the blink of an eye, the planes bombed our neighbor's house. They had been preparing to flee trying to escape death, but death was faster. A relative called and asked us to come to his shop, a clothing store near al-Shifa Hospital. There was no time to think. We began our journey, the journey of suffering and pain, the journey of fear, the journey of death.

My grandfather had a car and so did one of my uncles. We decided to put the children in the two cars and for the rest to go on foot. We left our street and reached the main road where the first shock awaited us: a scene from the Day of Judgement.

The street was overflowing with people, everyone was running, no one knew where to go. They were fleeing death to the unknown. As we walked, suddenly the planes targeted the central market. The place was turned into scattered body parts and corpses of people who a moment earlier had been trying to escape.

I froze in place, my hands were trembling, a chill shot down my spine. I stared at the massacre before my dull eyes. Then I heard my father, who squeezed my hand, say:

"We are totally helpless, son. If you stay here you will be like them, your torn limbs will mix with theirs."

It was the terrifying truth.

We continued on our way, death close at our heels. Two hours later, we arrived at al-Shifa Hospital where we met up with my grandfather and the children. They rushed toward us, embracing us with eyes full of tears. We had been apart for only two hours, but those were unlike any two hours we knew, two hours of hell.

In that cramped space we found clothes and bedding. I asked my grandmother, "Where did this come from? We brought nothing with us."

She smiled and said, "There is still good in this world. When our car arrived, the people of the neighborhood welcomed us. They competed with each other in offering help. Each one came with all they could carry from their home."

My people are great and generous despite everything they endure.

That night the planes never stopped bombing, the ground never stopped trembling, my heart never stopped palpitating—absolute terror. I will never forget that feeling.

At three o'clock in the morning, my father received a phone call. When the call ended, he was silent for two minutes, then he called me to say that my grandmother had been martyred. "We have to tell your mother."

I could not control myself; I burst out crying. My mother hurried over to comfort me:

"What's wrong? What happened? Why are you crying?"

Stunned, I did not know what to say. My father held her by the shoulders and told her, broken and weeping: "Your mother has been martyred!"

What happened next, I cannot describe to you.

My mother collapsed.

She had always been a source of strength; but that moment was the first time I saw my mother broken.

Hours later, while we were trying to comfort each other, my father received another call. It was the same person who had informed him of my grandmother's martyrdom. He stepped outside and returned a minute later with conflicted tears on his face, tears of sorrow on his cheeks and tears of joy in his eyes. He choked out the words, "The news was wrong. Your grandmother is alive."

It was as if life had been breathed into us again, but our joy did not last for long. He spoke again, faintly, "But in that strike, twenty-two people were martyred. Two entire families were wiped off the civil registry in an instant."[1]

✾ ✾ ✾ ✾ ✾

---

1   According to the government information office in Gaza, about 2,200 Palestinian families, including their entire members across generations, were erased from the civil registry between the beginning of the war on October 7, 2023, and May 2025. This number, along with the existing statistics documenting the genocide, is incomplete as tens of thousands of Palestinians remain missing in Gaza, researchers are unable to keep up with the death toll, and journalists are deliberately targeted and killed.

At sunrise, I went with my uncle to buy bread. We took a short-cut through al-Shifa Hospital.[2] It felt as though we'd passed through a gateway into a different world, a world where pain never stops, with no end of ambulances arriving, carrying life-less bodies inside. The place was overcrowded with moans and screams.

My mind felt empty—shock had paralyzed my thoughts. As we exited through the hospital's back gate, a man called out to us with a weak, broken voice:

"Hey guys . . . you with the bread, wait! I need your help."

I turned around and saw him dragging his injured leg. His other leg was fine, but in order to walk he had to carry his injured leg with his torn hands so that it could keep up with its sister.

"If you please, come . . . " he said, exhausted. "Carry the body of my niece from the morgue refrigerator and help me find a car so that I can take her to the cemetery and bury her."

We carried the body for him, a small lifeless body. I trembled out of fear. It was the first time in my life that I had held a corpse. As we walked, I asked him innocently, "Why are you alone? Why didn't anyone come with you?"

He stopped and his tears rained down. "There is no one left," he choked. "My brother and his family were martyred yesterday.

---

2   Al-Shifa Hospital is the largest medical complex in Gaza. In March 2024, it was the scene of the greatest massacre at a medical facility in history. Occupation forces bombed, burnt, and bulldozed various hospital departments and the surrounding neighborhood, including a building containing the largest stock of medicine in Gaza. Dozens were executed in the field and buried in mass graves, including women and the elderly as well as the wounded. Some were stripped of their clothes and had their hands tied before being executed. Over the following months, mass graves were discovered at the hospital. The prosecuting attorney at the International Criminal Court requested an investigation of this massacre perpetrated by the occupation forces.

Only this little girl and I escaped. But death insisted on taking her too . . . My relatives are far away and are unable to come because of the bombing and the dangers on the roads."

He got into the front seat, and we laid out the child's body on the back seat. I stared at her, a body motionless, voiceless, lifeless . . . A child robbed of her childhood, of a peaceful life, a gentle death, even of mourners who would bid her farewell in a funeral she deserved.

On that day, I did not eat, drink, or sleep. I was in shock. I felt like my skull was empty of thought, nothing was running through my mind besides one thought: *What is this injustice!*

That evening, as the bombing intensified, I felt that in this situation, we could not stand idly by. My uncle and I went to the hospital to help in any way we could.

My uncle's idea was to go to the morgue. When we arrived, we were shocked by a truly appalling scene: An overwhelming number of corpses! Bodies piled up in every corner. The dead outnumbered the living. All you could smell was blood and death . . . The smell of burnt human flesh.

We got to work.

We carried corpses from ambulances to the morgue where there was an attempt to identify the martyrs, and from there to wash and wrap them in shrouds.

It was indescribable,

bodies with no heads,

bodies with no limbs,

limbs of children,

crushed skulls,

crushed limbs . . .

Most bodies could not be identified. Sometimes there were only dismembered bodies or bodies burned like coal that no longer had any features. To identify the bodies, the staff of the morgue would first look at the face; if that was insufficient, they looked at the clothes the corpse was wearing. Often, there were no full bodies, only body parts. In that case, they would gather what seems to belong together into a single bag, then weigh it. Based on the weight, they estimate whether the victim was a child, a youth, or an adult.

Can you imagine what I'm saying! This is happening to human beings like yourself on the same planet you live on.

I will never forget one scene from that day when a young man came to identify the body of his brother. The staff member asked him:

"What does your brother look like?"

He said through tears: "White face, blond beard, tall, and blue eyes."

After a long search he found his brother. But there was nothing recognizable left of his face or eyes. His face had been crushed; all that remained was his chin with the burned remnants of his beard.

He hugged his brother's corpse and kissed his beard. His tears merged with his brother's blood. He sobbed, "We shall meet in heaven, my brother, promise me that. I'll see you again, right?"

Another scene I recall from that painful day was the massacre in al-Shati refugee camp; their damned planes wiped out an entire block, and the affection of those who loved it. The number of martyrs of that massacre reached seventy-two people. After we had shrouded the martyrs: children, women, old, young and middle-aged men, all corpses, all of them dead!—we placed them near the door to the refrigerated room in the morgue awaiting transport to the cemetery.

Do you know how they were transported?

A large truck used to transport vegetables arrived and those pure bodies were placed inside it to be buried. Those pure corpses were placed in the vegetable truck on the way to burial.

We in Gaza have been deprived of literally everything, even of a burial ceremony worthy of human beings—that is what I find most painful. But we are confident that God will honor them in Paradise; I am certain that young man will meet his brother in Paradise; certain that young girl will be happy there, that the inhabitants of that block will be gathered there. Sufficient is the injustice we have endured in this world. I hope we will find compensation in the next.

Two days after we had settled near al-Shifa Hospital, the monsters smelled the scent of life again. Their threats grew louder, and their damned army approached. We reached a consensus: we had to head south of the valley, specifically to the city of Deir al-Balah in the central province.

By exactly 6:00 a.m., we had packed our belongings into our cars and a taxi we had rented. We climbed into the vehicles, following a routine that only the people of Gaza understand. Let me explain:

The first car carried my grandfather, one of my uncles, and my brothers; the second car carried my grandmother, myself, and the wife and children of my uncle. Do you know why that was? So that someone would remain to carry the family name, as we expected death at any moment. In Gaza, we are surrounded by the possibility of death.

The question in our minds was not whether we would live or die, but how the monsters would kill us. All of us hoped to die a quick death without much suffering and pain. We hoped our bodies would remain in one piece after being bombed.

We followed the coastal al-Rashid Road.[3] I will never forget that day. A warship was sailing in our sea like a monster, an instrument of death and destruction. My heart aches, as I try to recall the situation now, remembering those moments when I expected to die.

I saw death before me, all along that road. I was in the middle car, so I kept looking to the front and the rear to check on my family. I kept turning my head so as not to see those monsters invading our sea. I had only two scenarios in mind: one in which I was collecting the remains of my family, and another where

---

3   Al-Rashid Road is considered one of the two main roads in the Gaza Strip, running from the south to the north. The other is Salah al-Din Road, the main highway in the Gaza Strip, which had been the scene of the historic return of the people of Gaza to the north during the January-March 2025 ceasefire.

they were collecting mine. I anticipated the burning ball of death which would turn me into charred remains; I awaited a cursed projectile that would turn me into the sole survivor.

The cannons of death were aimed in our direction. Around that cursed warship lay their remaining supporting vessels painted pitch black, their color, the color of their deeds.

I felt the sea in those moments, felt its anger, sorrow, and irritation. I felt its rejection of reality. Yes, I felt it. It is our sea, our endowment. Everything on this land is ours and we belong to the land. They are tyrants who are strong but whose day will come, like all the others. History is proof of that.

We finally arrived at our destination, an UNRWA[4] school, which had not been designated as a shelter at that time.

We had no choice. We opened up the school and were its first residents. We moved the student desks from one classroom into the school courtyard and sat down. Then the questions started: what are we to do?

Or rather, what will they do to us?

---

4   The United Nations Relief and Works Agency for Palestine Refugees. UNRWA has since 1948 been an essential pillar in the survival of Palestinian refugees, offering services such as education, medical treatment, and general welfare. In the decades since the Nakba, its legitimacy has been attacked relentlessly by Israel, culminating in a number of Western nations, lead among them the US, cutting funding for UNRWA thus further squeezing the livelihoods and well-being of Palestinian refugees.

It is not uncommon for United Nations facilities to be used as shelters by local populations in dire times, such as the case in Qana in southern Lebanon during Israel's Operation Grapes of Wrath in 1996, where Israeli artillery bombardment killed more than a hundred civilians seeking shelter in a UN compound. Likewise, UNRWA facilities were used as shelter by displaced Palestinians during the ongoing genocide in Gaza.

None of us had an answer, not my seventy-year-old grandfather, not my grandmother, or my father or mother, or my uncles and their wives, or our children.

The only reality at the time was the unknown, nothing but the unknown or death, and both were bitter.

The sun set and night fell, but it did not turn dark because the sky was still bright. In the Arabic language, the word *noor*, or light, carries connotations of goodness and blessings and peace. But for us in Gaza, the connotations have been reversed: light means that lives have been lost, bodies have been dismembered, houses have been destroyed. Light here only signifies death. It is the flame of their accursed shells, it is the light that kills our dreams and ends our lives.

We entered the classroom we had chosen with care; it was on the ground floor at the northern edge of the school. We avoided the center out of fear of random missiles from the west fired from their wretched ships or from the east from their damned artillery. We chose a ground floor classroom, based on the calculation that we stood a better chance of survival than if we had chosen a higher floor, in case the school was bombed.

Yes, this is our logic—this is how we think. In Gaza, with every step you take, you must factor in death. For here, death is everywhere, at any time, in everything.

Do you know how we slept that night?

All we had were two blankets which had to serve as bedding for twenty children. We found curtains in classrooms which served as bedding for my grandparents. As for the rest, my father and mother and my uncles and their wives, they had nothing. The cold, fear, and anxiety were their blankets. I was lucky that I even had a mattress!

My mattress consisted of the floor mats in my grandfather's car and my cover was a magazine with a well-known poem written in it: "We Shall Return to Jaffa" by a celebrated Palestinian poet who had died before he could return.

A fear came over me that I would share his fate. The poem was written in 1948 and yet the Nakba continues to this day. Their barbaric mentality and agenda have not changed; they only know killing and the expulsion of populations and the theft of property. I fear that one day I'll write: "We Shall Return to Beit Hanoun."

I fear I won't even get the chance to write it.

I fear I will be killed before I even live.

That was the first night I felt defeated, powerless, weak. Covers for our children—we couldn't even provide those.

It was the first night in the south of the valley.[5]

It was also the first night in a series of displacements.

---

5   South of the Gaza Valley. The Israeli army of occupation announced on Saturday October 14, 2023 that the population of northern Gaza were to be forcibly moved and that they should head south, a measure which the United Nations has described as a crime against humanity.

The following morning their threats increased and the displacement of those wanting to live grew, as did those going from the north of the valley to the south. People flocked to the school like innocent birds searching for security, birds running from the rifles of death, birds fleeing the crows of destruction.

By midday, the school was full of the displaced, people from all parts of Gaza, people who had left everything behind—their homes, possessions, lands—and who were now looking for security.

The school was full of thousands of trembling hearts, thousands who were lost in the unknown. The question occupying everyone's minds, old and young, men and women, was what is to be our fate?

What will happen to us?

That day, a UNRWA car arrived with a few supervisors, and the school was officially recognized as an affiliated shelter.

As evening fell, local families began to arrive carrying all the supplies they could. They shared everything they had: their clothes, their bedding, their food . . . Pure generosity, deep compassion, incredible unity . . . Truly, we are a people who deserve life. Our poet Mahmoud Darwish was right when he said: "We have on this land that which makes life worth living." We deserve life, we love life, we are the children of life.

That scene represented hope amidst the destruction, life amidst death. We were like a small phoenix trying everything it can to dig out of the mound of debris above it.

To you, the one reading these words . . . know this:

As I write now, I cry. As I try to recall what happened to me, I cry. For your information, a year and four months has passed since what I've written about all started, and yet my suffering continues. I am still displaced, still waiting for death. What forces me to stay up until this late hour of the night is my fear of sleeping, my fear of my painful reality. I sit on my knees, on my bedding, inside my tent, surrounded by my family. Every word I write I expect could be my last. The bombing doesn't stop. The death doesn't end. Here in Gaza, all you'll find is death.

I will start to close this chapter here. I will call it "My Journey from Home to Tent," about the first displacement journey from the north to the south of the valley. The title does not matter much. In truth, nothing I write really matters. Because, if you want the honest truth: we don't matter, we have no value in the scales of this unjust world. If the world saw us as human beings, our extermination would have stopped long ago. But even with all of this, I will continue writing. I'll keep writing until I find something to escape my nightmares. To escape the missile that chases me in my sleep. To escape the ghosts of my loved ones . . . whom the monsters have annihilated.

As the Zionists penetrated deeper into the Gaza Strip, the number of displaced people from the north of the strip to the south also grew. At that time, to be precise, two days after our arrival at the school, the number of displaced living in each classroom had risen to sixty. I was lucky because there weren't too many people in the classroom where my family and I were staying, only fifty-two people: thirty-six from my family, a second family with nine members, and a third family of seven people.

Yes, you read that right!! A five-by-ten-meter classroom housing fifty-two people. Each of us had a share of less than one square meter.

Then the tents began to appear!

In truth, they are not worthy of being called tents. They are more like patchwork assemblies held together by nails and screws to provide some privacy, no more. They were made up of wooden boards and iron rods covered by cloth or nylon, a covering stitched together out of what was available to provide privacy to those within. They did not protect from the heat of summer or the cold and rain of winter.

People squatted in every government department, every school, hospital courtyard, nursery, university, and any vacant bit of land, even the sidewalks. The playground of the school I was in was filled up with tents, even the rear courtyard which was no more than two meters wide. The classroom in which we were staying turned into a dark graveyard, with the front filled with tents; people had covered the windows overlooking the rear courtyard to give them some semblance of privacy. Our lives were an indescribable tragedy. The number of residents of the school reached twenty thousand. I would also like you to know that the school had only ten toilets; by a simple calculation, that's two thousand people per toilet.

Can you imagine?! Yes, that was our reality.

It was natural that you would find yourself in the queue behind twenty people in order to get use of that damned toilet for two or three minutes. Answering the call of nature became a major concern. The occupation forces had made suffering an essential part of our daily routine. I used to have to stay up till one in the morning to enter the bathroom to avoid that loathsome line.

After several days of living in that narrow classroom, the situation became unbearable; the situation at the school became more complicated, sanitation was a constant problem. Several attempts to improve matters failed. We had to find somewhere more private.

My father decided that we should erect a tent outside the school. He began by collecting the necessities: leftover planks of wood, metal supports, part of the cloth and nylon he had bought from a place nearby. It took my father a few hours to obtain and prepare the materials. He tied the pieces of wood with some metal wires he had found, and he covered the structure with the cloth we had been able to acquire, and he used the sheet of nylon for a roof. It was a small, simple tent, but it became our refuge. It provided some privacy, and we spent our days there. That was the first time in almost two weeks that I was able to take a shower.

Dear Reader,

I've walked you through this journey from Beit Hanoun to al-Shifa Hospital and then the south, from my home to my tent, from the bosom of my family to exile within my homeland, but even after all this I feel that my story alone is insufficient. I wrote this in order to tell what I had seen, what I had lived through, what I bled from my heart and my memory—but in truth, this war has never been my story alone.

Every face I have encountered, every tent I passed by, every eye into which I have gazed, all have stories no less painful than mine. I feel it would be unjust to confine the narrative to only what I had seen. Pain has suffused the whole place. Suffering and sorrow are to be found in every street, every corner, and every tent.

That is why I have decided to continue this book in a different way. I will write, yes, but not just about myself. I will open the coming pages to many voices, to faces that the cameras never reached, to suffering that was never told, to details that shake the heart more than explosions. I will write each chapter as if it were a witness in a court of justice, a witness to the Zionists' barbarity and crimes. I will write every word as though it were a tombstone, a grave marker for Gaza. I will write every sentence as though it were a cry for help from hell, a cry from a weak, hungry, terrified human being, drowning in the unknown, in suffering and sorrow.

I will begin with the most extreme of what we lived through, those days when bread became a dream and food a wish . . .

I will begin a new chapter.
I shall name it "Hunger and Bread."

Hunger and Bread

After the first month of the aggression, hunger became their most dangerous weapon. I had never imagined that a day would come when bread would be a treasure. I never thought that I would see the elderly splitting a small piece of bread among them, or children crying, not because they had lost a toy, but because starvation was tormenting them and there was nothing to ease their pain and hunger.

I never thought I would see innocent tears on the cheeks of my sleeping brother because we did not have anything to tame the wild beast of hunger gnawing at his insides.

It began silently. The store shelves emptied, bakeries shut their doors, people tried to put aside flour, rice, or anything edible that was left.

As the days went by and the Zionists penetrated deeper into Gaza, there was nothing left in the markets. Signs of famine began to appear, and our days were divided into long lines: one line for bread, another for water, and a third for a can of tuna. Each meal became simply a means of survival. Ironically, I had once thought that death was the scariest thing, but in that moment, death was the most merciful and compassionate thing a person could experience.

We were growing weaker, fading, breaking slowly. In this chapter I shall talk about hunger and its physical pain . . . the unseen side of war. I shall speak of the greatest human humiliation of this century.

I shall begin with myself. In those difficult days, my extended family (everyone who has my grandfather's name) resorted to a unique mutual agreement that almost resembled a primitive socialist model. We chose one of our uncles to be responsible for us all and put our money in his hands, leaving it up to him to provide for our needs. He bought a large pot, two sacks of rice, and five sacks of flour, in addition to some beans and legumes. My mother was in charge of cooking.

Thirty-six individuals ate food cooked in that pot. The distribution was as follows: every four individuals got one plateful and each individual got one piece of bread a day. We organized ourselves like this not out of choice, but out of a necessity imposed on us by reality. The main reason for adopting this system was the disparity in our living conditions, and it was our way of easing the burden on each other and standing together against poverty and war.

As the days went by, the proportion of water in the pot increased and the individual portions decreased. We started to improvise new types of food and substitutes for missing ingredients in recipes. For example, we used seawater to compensate for the lack of salt. Imagine!

We went through a period in which there was no real food to be had. I remember one potato stew—that wasn't really stew; it was more like water and water, then more water, and just a little tomato sauce and a few barely-visible bits of diced potato floating in a giant pot.

I remember my cousin, a three-year-old child, who would take his daily share of bread, one small piece—baked in a rudimentary mud oven that burned discarded plastic and nylon as fuel, emitting noxious and sickening fumes—and hold onto it all day long. He would eat half of it for lunch and keep the other irreplaceable half for dinner, never letting it out of his hands out of fear he might lose it, scared he would get hungry at night and not find anything to mollify his stomach. He would go hungry all day long, clutching the bread in his hand, just so that he could sleep through the night.

For many days our lunch was rice—the worst kind of rice—or that stew. I don't know if I could really call it cooking, because in fact it was just boiled water (a lot of water is boiled on a disease-emitting fire of burning trash and suffocating odors).

Those were difficult days, cruel and painful days. Days which robbed grown-ups of their esteem and dignity, and children of their innocence and spontaneity.

In reality, there was wood—there were groves of trees near the school—however, the price for that wood was our lives. At the beginning of our stay, my uncles and I used to go there. But what stopped us from going again, forcing us to stop and switch to using plastic and other toxic fuel, was because of something that happened to me.

I went by myself to a grove at nine o'clock in the morning while my father and uncles were standing in the line for water. We had agreed that I would go ahead on my own and collect as much firewood as I could, and as soon as they finished filling the water they would join me to help carry the wood. But just as I was about to go into the grove, I found myself directly in front of a battleship. I remember that very well. I stood and stared at those cursed military vessels which had come closer to shore. I looked at them with fear, powerless. I was afraid they would fire on me. There was no one around to save me.

Then suddenly, an F-16 plane began bombing the groves, right in front of me.[1] The ground beneath me shook, tree roots were flying towards me along with shrapnel and sand. I froze: my legs

---

1   By May 2025, more than 95 percent of Gaza's total agricultural lands have been destroyed or are unusable, including greenhouses and agricultural wells. The director-general of the Food and Agricultural Organization claimed that "this level of destruction is not just a loss of infrastructure—it is a collapse of Gaza's agrifood system and of lifelines."

could not support me, my heart's palpitations grew louder, my hands were shaking, my lips quivering. I had expected death to come from the direction of the sea, but it fell from the sky instead. I was so frightened I was unable to run; I could barely walk.

On my way back, I saw my father and uncles approaching from a distance. I felt a wave of relief—finally, someone to save me. I waved at them, they saw me and started running towards me . . .

. . . suddenly, I woke up to the sound of them yelling: "Wasim, Wasim . . . Wake up, Wasim."

They picked me up and I threw one arm around my father and another around one of my uncles and we made our way towards the school.

My mother met us at the entrance to the school and she hugged me tightly. Her terrified heartbeat shook my body, but I was paralyzed with fear. She kept repeating: "We don't want any firewood, my son, we do not want to eat." After that we decided to go with plastic. Poison is better than death.

*****

By the fortieth day of the genocide, our store of food and flour was exhausted. All that was left were two meals of rice. We began to search. We had only two days.

The Nuseirat Camp[2] is near the Gaza Valley where the Zionists established a barrier that separates the north from the south.[3] There was a grain mill there and if you brought a sack of wheat and ten liters of diesel, you could get one sack of flour.

But do you think that was easy?!

Do you think getting diesel and wheat in Gaza was simple?!

To get the wheat, we went to a granary in Deir al-Balah. The main doors were shut, and people were entering through a small side door. They were on top of each other, pushing to enter as though they were pushing to enter paradise—I would not be exaggerating if I were to say that it felt like paradise was inside, life and salvation were inside.

My uncles and I got into formation: I went in front, one uncle pushed people away on my right, another pushed people away from my left and a third pushed me forward from behind. After

---

2   Established in 1948 after the Nakba, Nuseirat is the third largest refugee camp in Palestine in terms of area and population after Jabalia and al-Shati. It is situated in the middle of the Gaza Strip. The camp was subject to several campaigns of Israeli aerial bombardments during the genocide, and appalling massacres of civilians were perpetrated there by the Israeli Air Force. It was also the scene of fierce battles between the occupation forces and the Palestinian resistance.

3   The Netzarim Corridor divides Gaza City and areas to the north from the south of the Strip and is named after a prominent Jewish settlement which was dismantled after the liberation of Gaza in 2005. The barrier had a strategic use in forced migration and siege during the genocide, and was used by the occupation forces as a site where sniping crimes were committed. Documented witness accounts show that Israeli troops fired on Palestinians whose bodies were dragged and left in the open air. The corridor turned into a scene of bloody confrontations where the Palestinian resistance was able to inflict serious casualties on the army of occupation. The barrier turned it into a strategic liability which led to its dismantling during the January 2025 ceasefire and the return of people to the north. The Netzarim Corridor became a symbol of Israeli crimes and Palestinian steadfastness.

a lot of effort and a lot of pushing, the uncle to my right and I managed to get in.

There was a long line inside extending all the way to the back where there was a wooden desk on which was written "The Company Accountant." On the wall behind him a sign was posted in thick black letters: "Prices are final and nonnegotiable; every family gets only one sack." Near the desk there was a pile of sacks of wheat.

We stood in line. My gaze and interest were focused on that pile of bags. My uncle was praying:

"God, oh, God, please don't let the wheat run out before we get our share."

As he and I were expressing our joy and sense of accomplishment we were interrupted by one of the workers who called out:

"Close the door. The remaining wheat is barely enough for those already inside."

My other uncles were unable to enter. My joy evaporated, I panicked. What did that employee mean by there is hardly enough for those inside?

My uncle called to inform me in a pained and sad tone that they had not been to get in. "Perhaps it isn't so bad," he said. "Two sacks of wheat are better than nothing."

I responded: "Pray harder. One of the workers here says the wheat is barely enough for those inside." A long groan and the discussion ended.

My eyes anxiously monitored that pile of sacks: *Will we get some? Or will they run out before it is my turn?* As each sack was given away, I lost a bit of my soul. I was thinking of my father and mother, my grandfather and grandmother, our children, and my little cousin, the owner of the piece of bread I told you about. *Will we be able to feed them? Will they get to eat bread? Will our hunger persist?*

After nearly half an hour, the last sack was gone. We could hear voices raised in protest, voices of the hungry, voices of people concerned for their children's starvation.

There were about twenty people in the storeroom. We all thought we should not leave until we got some wheat. The workers tried to evict us by force; we raised our voices, which forced them to retreat and be quiet. After nearly an hour and a half of waiting, the accountant came and informed us that all the company had left was ten sacks, so each person could have half a sack. As I write to you now, I'm smiling, a smile from the heart. I remember that feeling that overcame me in that moment, overwhelming joy. My heart danced. "*Alhamdullilah*, praise be to God," my uncle repeated in a loud voice. "*Alhamdullilah*."

My share was half a sack, the same for my uncle. We received one sack, what you could call our trophy. I felt I was carrying a sack of souls, not grains of wheat.

We left the storehouse quickly. We were about three kilometers from the school but we did not pause for even a second to consider how we would get back—in fact, we did not feel tired; our joy dominated everything else.

With each step we took on the way back, we encountered questions:

"Where did you get the wheat?"

"What does it cost?"

"Is there anymore?"

"Do you want to sell it?"

And every inquiring eye sparkled with hope, but sadly, that hope quickly faded with the answer . . .

We had fulfilled the first task. What remained, obtaining the diesel, was the hardest part. At that time all gas stations had run out of fuel and were closed. Diesel was being sold on the black market. It was like buying drugs; getting to the sellers was incredibly dangerous and it was even more dangerous to deal with them.

After a lengthy search we were told that at exactly 10 p.m. a car came along the corniche near a well-known intersection and sold diesel.

Do you know what it feels like to walk on the street at ten o'clock at night under those circumstances? Whoever went out at that time was sentencing himself to death. But our need was urgent. We decided to take the risk. It helped that the location was not far from the school.

By 9:30 p.m. we were in position at the specified location. We waited for about an hour, an hour of fear and anxiety, an hour of terror and expectation of death. At exactly 10:40 p.m. the vehicle arrived, and we bought diesel from it at nine times the normal price. It was the first time in my life dealing with merchants of death and suffering—war profiteers—partners with the Zionists in our extermination.

Only the final task remained, going to the Nuseirat mill. At the crack of dawn the following day we rented a donkey cart. We began our journey armed with the wheat and diesel. After an hour we reached the mill where we found a very, very long line. Everyone would deliver their wheat and diesel to the mill, whereupon they would be given a receipt guaranteeing them the right to a sack of flour after two days.

On our way back, we couldn't stop talking: "Finally, we'll get flour." "Finally, our children will eat!" But my uncle interrupted us, saying, "But what will we feed the kids in the meantime? We have nothing left. The rice we cooked yesterday was our last meal . . . "

As we came upon the school, we passed a tent at the entrance belonging to one of my grandfather's relatives. As soon as he saw us, he shouted in surprise: "Where is the flour? What happened?"

"They told us we'll get it in two days," my uncle replied.

My grandfather's relative interrupted: "Well maybe it's for the best. Take my flour for now, make do for these two days, and give it back when you get yours."

Moments like that bring me peace. There are many among us who still hold on to generosity and kindness . . . Despite everything, goodness still lives in us. Two days later we received our sack of flour, the cure to hunger, white gold . . .

Upon our return to the school, the welcome ceremony started, the royal coronation ceremony. The children surrounded us dancing and singing with joy: "Flour, flour!" My grandfather's relative called out: "Congratulations, congratulations, guys. *Alhamdullilah.*" When we got to the classroom, we found my father and mother, my grandmother and grandfather, the wives of my uncles, all standing at the door, their eyes shining bright, with beaming smiles, heads held high. Everyone was exclaiming, *"Alhamdullilah. Alhamdullilah.* Finally."

When I saw them, I felt the rush of victory, delight in winning.

As soon as we sat down, my mother immediately lit the fire and began making coffee as a reward for our achievement. Sitting next to my mother I remembered myself, I remembered who I was, I remembered that I was that university student passionate about the sciences and physics. I remembered my family being a cultured and educated family.

Has flour become a dream and an achievement for us? Has the calamity led us to this point?

Dear reader,

As I write to you now, a year and a half later during the spring of 2025, the Zionists have returned to complete our extermination. I'm suffering from a crippling food crisis. The crossings have been closed for fifty days and famine looms. All that we have is about half a sack of flour.

A year and a half of our lives have passed, and now one of our greatest dreams is having a sack of flour. Flour had never been something we thought about, but now that same flour consumes our thoughts and dreams and aspirations. My dream of being an explorer of this universe has been replaced, buried by the dream of securing a sack of flour . . .

In that period, the first round of negotiations between the two sides began and led to a temporary ceasefire, "The First Cease-fire."[4] It began at dawn on the fifty-fifth day of the genocidal war and lasted seven days during which the points of entry were opened for humanitarian aid, the essential supplies for hospitals, and some medical delegations.

I remember well how we crowded around my grandfather as he held his radio in both his hands as though he was cradling his own heart. We awaited the moment of the ceasefire announcement as though it was the moment of a new birth, the birth of hope, life, and security.

As the news broadcast began, everyone looked at each other with eyes filled with a thousand questions and a thousand wishes—all afraid of disappointment.

Suddenly, before anything was said, the children began repeating a chant they had just made up on the spot: "Ceasefire! Ceasefire!" My grandfather lifted the radio to his ear and waved his other arm in the air asking for silence so he could hear the news.[5] It took only a few seconds for him to join the children in their joy as he repeated in his tired voice: "Ceasefire, ceasefire, *alhamdullilah!*"

---

4   The first ceasefire lasted for seven days, beginning on November 24, 2023, which included an exchange of prisoners and the entry of truckloads of aid to Gaza.

5   Wasim's grandfather, Abu Tariq, was born in Beit Hanoun in 1953. He has the equivalent of a Bachelor's degree in education with a major in English from al-Azhar University in Egypt. He began his career as a teacher at the Beit Hanoun Agricultural School where he worked for four years, then he moved to Saudi Arabia where he pursued his career as a teacher for eighteen years. He returned to the Gaza Strip in 2001 and continued teaching and moving from school to school until his retirement. He spent most of his days during the genocide reading the Qur'an and devoted calm moments listening to songs by Farid al-Atrash. What bothered him the most while living in his tent were stories about forced migration. He often repeats his slogan: "I'd rather be under a tree in Beit Hanoun than anywhere else in the world."

The sounds of celebrations erupted in the school. Everyone was happy. That was the first time I saw smiles on the faces of displaced people with me in that school. It breathed new life into us. We hoped that was the beginning of the end of the genocide.

It is true, nevertheless, that returning to the north was still forbidden, but we would be eating at last.

We made our first decision: "Bake all the flour we have—and tonight, we'll eat till we're full."

As the ceasefire came into effect, signs of improvement spread in the details of our lives, like veins pumping blood again after a long coma. The price of flour suddenly dropped, and we began to see chicken and meat on the market once again as though they had returned to apologize for their absence; bakeries opened their doors, fruits and vegetables began to flood the markets, restoring life in the eyes of the weary. Even cooking gas became available, and one could smell delicious aromas wafting out classroom windows and in the alleys between tents.

In those seven days, I experienced a sensation that my soul had not experienced in a long time. Gratitude filled my heart to the brim, like standing in the rain after a long thirst. Like embracing my children after a long separation. Like a parched palm tree revived by water.

But the greatest feeling was the sense of security we felt: found on the faces of sleeping children not crying, in the silence that replaced the sound of rockets, in the clinking of spoons scraping against plates instead of the sound of rubble flying by, the pervasive smell of bread and chicken, the sound of laughter from the heart, not strained by danger and terror.

That sensation was not just the absence of fear—it was life restored.

But those days were like everything beautiful in Gaza. It didn't last.

The seven days ended as a beautiful dream ended at the harsh sound of an alarm clock.

We hardly felt them, they passed like a warm minute in a cold lifetime. Suddenly everything went backwards. Death knocked on our doors again—no, it demolished them.

The feeling of security, which had started to grow like a small sprout of coriander in the heaps of rubble, was pulled up by the roots and withered away.

The sound of bombing resumed, as though someone had pressed the repeat button. The crossings slammed shut again, as if they had opened only to let us taste life so that we would yearn for it more when it was snatched away.

The lump in our throats returned and fear spread once more to all reaches of the school, among the tents and in the eyes of the children. We went back to counting our breaths, not knowing if we could complete them or if we would choke in the middle.

The bakeries continued to function thanks to the support of the World Food Programme[6] which supplied them with flour and diesel on condition that they sell the bread at a symbolic price no more than the cost of production. A package of bread weighing about three kilograms would sell for four shekels, which is equivalent to one U.S. dollar. However, the real price was not paid in currency but in hours of fatigue and waiting and sweating and fear—and sometimes in blood.

---

6   The UN World Food Programme (WFP) announced in May 2025 that half a
     million Palestinians in Gaza were under threat of starvation, and during the time
     in which Wasim was writing the famine reached new heights.

In Deir al-Balah alone there were nearly a million people, but the town had only three bakeries. Within less than a month, one of them was flattened by a surprise bombardment, so that we had only two bakeries left. Two bakeries for a million hungry mouths.

The queues were endless. The head of the line was like a mirage. You'd reach what you thought was the end, only to find many people still ahead of you.

At first, I would leave at dawn, walk an hour to the bakery, then walk another half an hour to join the back of the queue.

I stood there for long hours, until nightfall. The queue didn't move forward, it only moved backwards. Each time I stood in that damned line, I came back with no bread, returning with only hunger for my siblings.

At the bakery gate, there was no "queue," just a battlefield.

Bodies clashing, arms pushing, screams rising, cursing, children suffocating between legs. I saw men being beaten and falling. You couldn't breach that crowd on your own—you needed a group, a team, even a gang . . . just to reach the tiny iron window where bundles of bread were tossed like potions of salvation, as doses of life's elixirs.

One evening, my father, uncles, and I held an emergency (and hungry) meeting. We arrived at the conclusion that we should form a team (like the one I told you about on wheat day) and bind together in those dire battles that raged around the window to obtain life savers. We were forced to do that unless we wanted our children to go to sleep with empty bellies and weeping eyes.

Our team set off at the crack of dawn the following day. As soon as we reached the bakery, or the "battlefield," we engaged.

We pushed with all our strength, coordinating, searching for the weakest spot, and focusing our force to break through the colliding human wall. In the midst of that battle, other battles broke out elsewhere, in my mind and thoughts, a battle between who I used to be and who I had become. What was I doing? Fighting people for bread? Is this what a university student, a so-called intellectual, does? Didn't I have a duty to be a role model?

I want to get out of there. I do not want the bread.

I want to remain as I used to be, not be transformed into a beast.

I shall set an example as I used to.

Suddenly I remembered my brother who went to sleep in tears the previous night because of his hunger and his empty stomach.

The sound of his moans and grumbling stomach sounded in my head like thunder.

It shattered all my thoughts. I wanted nothing now, except bread. I just wanted to feed my brothers.

I pulled myself together. I dug my foot into the ground and pushed my body forward in the direction of the small iron window.

Finally, I got there. I extended my hand, joy bursting into flame within me as I saw that worker sorting the loaves of bread dancing on the oven's conveyor belt. Finally, they were in my hands!

I wanted to get out, but there was no way to go back, things only moved forward. Yet after a long and difficult struggle, just like the one I had gone through, I made an exit. I left the battlefield victorious with the bread in my hands.

I lifted the bread over my head like an Olympic trophy and I called out to my father, sitting on the other side of the sidewalk, in a voice full of joy: "Here's the bread, Dad! Here's the bread!" The spark in his eyes reflected the spark in mine. I shall never forget his smile as long as I live.

My uncles were still on the battlefield. I stood at the edge of the crowd and called out to them: "I got bread, I got a bundle!" One of them heard me and replied in a quavering voice resulting from the intense shoving: "Go back to the classroom and let the children eat breakfast."

My father and I returned together carrying the bread. On the way people congratulated us on our achievement.

We reached the classroom, and the usual welcome rituals began; everyone was happy, there was joy everywhere. My father began distributing the bread and each person received one whole piece, free of the smell of plastic. That bread was for breakfast only. We had been very generous in the distribution; the bread for lunch and dinner was secure as the rest of the fighters were still in battle.

In that period, it was not only hunger that was eating at our hearts; there was that sense of helplessness as you stopped in front of a small store and saw what you needed on display before you and you realized that you could not pay for it.

At the beginning of the war, you starved because the markets were empty. Now, food was available, but there was no money.

Those goods were on the market, as I explained to you previously, because they were allowed to enter during the first cease-fire. In reality, they were limited goods in quite small quantities.

Our hearts grew heavier and our pockets emptier day after day. One no longer heard the sound of sales being rung up in the market but the sounds of uncertainty and embarrassment. Our hands wished to grab anything to quell the hunger, to keep body and soul together. Yet our eyes avoided the prices.

In the midst of this, the *takiyat*[7] emerged as a life saver.

A *takiya* (singular), as people use the term, is a place where food is prepared and distributed for free to those in need. You are not asked your name, your line of work or how much you own. It is sufficient that hunger has led you there.

At the beginning the *takiyat* were individual and modest initiatives, cauldrons boiling in mosque courtyards or in front of homes, simple food that is sufficient to quell hunger.

Later, as the need increased, initiatives and societies sprang up supported by the free people of the world, to organize the effort and secure what is needed for its continuation.

Thus, the *takiyat* turned into another symbol of steadfastness, and a new scene in a city fighting to stay alive.

As the situation grew more desperate and the goods available on the market dwindled, anxiety spread more widely than ever before. The *takiyat*, which had been a simple recourse, now became a faint hope in a sea of despair. The quantity of food distributed was insufficient for the growing numbers of those in need. The food diminished from day to day while the hungry increased.

---

7   Communal kitchens are community-run facilities in Gaza where displaced Gazans collect simple meals like rice and lentils. A grassroots lifeline under blockade, *takiyat* were one of the last dependable food sources for hundreds of thousands during that phase of the genocide.

Long lines appeared at the doors of the *takiyat*, of people who had relinquished their dignity, whose bodies were exhausted so that they leaned against each other in heavy silence, with wary eyes, sweat covered brows, on feet tired from standing for long hours without knowing if they would get a share of the food that day or not. Waiting took a heavier toll than any other hardship.

Waiting which is all indignity, sorrow, and defeat.

Food in these *takiyat*, given all the needy and the limited food supply, became a rare commodity and an innocent dream.

At the doors of *takiyat* you will find hearts as empty of hope as their pockets were empty of money.

I paused at the door to a *takiya* and remembered that I was a student of physics. I had always been in search of answers to difficult questions. Today, however, I am searching for something much simpler. All I am looking for is a mouthful that will sate my hunger. Standing in the lines, I saw the breakdown in people's faces. Their eyes were telling silent stories. I was greatly moved. I felt that hunger wasn't just in people's bodies, it was in their souls too.

There were three lines. I stood in the middle line. After an hour of waiting, there were only four pots left, yet there were still hundreds of hungry people still in lines.

Chaos broke out. People left their positions in the queue and rushed to the distribution area, which was enclosed by iron bars embedded in the ground like prison bars, where there was a cement platform half a meter high, on which the large cooking pots were placed, with the workers standing behind it.

I took part in the rush.

Frail bodies pushed each other, each person hugging their share with both arms as if embracing their soul, afraid that it would be torn away in the crowd.

Arms were wrestling, containers bumping against our heads and faces, small children underfoot yelling; "Make room for us!" They did not want food, only escape from being trampled to death.

I pushed with my body until I reached the furthest point with my chest against the iron bars. I yelled at the top of my voice to the worker behind the bars: "Me . . . It's my turn!"

He was serving sorrow before the food, his face vanquished as he tried to feed everyone but could not.

He was looking at the faces, searching for who was hungriest so as to serve him first.

Finally, a ladle full of canned peas was poured into my container.

I braced the vessel against my stomach with all my might and began to walk backwards, trying to exit without burning myself or others with my food.

I got out . . . Finally, I was out.

I sat down along the side of the road, stretched out, gasping for breath, trying to calm down so that I would not lose consciousness.

I ate some of the food and watched the crowd of hungry people, the crowd of humiliation and anguish.

Suddenly . . . a nearby bombing.

What happened? Did the people run away?

No ... the crowd only grew.

Hunger knows no fear.

Amid the chaos, I heard men screaming: "The child is burned! The boy is burned!"

And behold: they brought out a little child whose face had melted ... his features had fused with each other from the extreme heat.

He was screaming in pain, out of fear and hunger, calling for his mother:

"*Yamma ... Yamma ...* "

They carried him and ran in the direction of the shelling where the ambulances were.

They carried the child and a heap of limbs.

I returned to school after that ...

I returned with food that tasted like a mix of pain, fear, and hunger.

Yet with all I had experienced, I knew I was fortunate compared to others.

In the north of the Gaza Strip, the pain was double, the hunger was fiercer, and death was closer.

There, life was not a struggle for daily bread, it was a struggle for one's very existence.

I was hearing stories that made my own suffering seem like luxury compared to what they went through . . . that made my hunger seem like a privilege. I shall now talk about them.

Here my story ends, and more heart-wrenching stories begin.

Stories of the Famine in the North

Uncle Abu Malek

My father's friend, Uncle Abu Malek, is a man in his forties. He supports his paraplegic mother who is in her seventies and two young children, both barely a year old. After twenty years of treatment, Abu Malek and his wife had finally been blessed with children—a small miracle after a lifetime of waiting.

When I talked to him about his story, he told me, "The situation here began to deteriorate quickly. There were no markets left, and there was nothing to eat. Whoever had a morsel hid it for his children.

"Fortunately, it was winter, and the land was covered with wild plants. The most important was *khobiza*, a green plant that we, the people of Gaza, are quite familiar with. It is part of a traditional warm dish in the winter, and we usually cook it with onions, dough, and spices.

"But this time there was nothing in the pot except for *khobiza*, chopped and boiled in water so that it turned into a tasteless sticky green soup. As time went by and as hunger intensified, flour disappeared altogether. There was no more bread, only a soupy drink with nothing to dip in it or fill you up with.

"This continued for almost a month, until a mill appeared in the Jabalia Camp where they ground yellow corn typically used as chicken feed and sold it as flour. Yes, we were reduced to eating rabbit food and chicken feed."

Abu Malek laughed, but his smile hid his heartbreak. "Things got better. Now we have something to dip in the *khobiza*: black pieces of bread that smell repulsive, but at least there is something to dip! We would devour that dish as though it was a luxurious feast—even though it was just wild plants and ground animal feed.

"Then the long-awaited news arrived: truckloads of flour were going to enter from the south to the north through al-Rashid Road, specifically near the Nabulsi Roundabout, what is now called Dawar Almout, or the 'Roundabout of Death.'

"At ten in the evening, I set out on foot with my team of seven men. We arrived an hour and a half later and gathered some pieces of wood from the rubble of the surrounding houses, starting a fire around which we could wait. There were ten of us there that night, seven men and three monsters that never left our side: hunger, fear, and the cold.

"We waited until nine in the morning. No trucks came. We went back to where we were staying, picking some wild plants we found growing along the way . . . the ingredients for another day's lunch of that cursed soup.

"Two days later, a new rumor: the trucks would enter that night. I did not believe it. Despair had taken hold of me. I was certain that I would be killed before I saw any flour. I stayed in the classroom while my friends went, but they had a car this time.

"At midnight, I was awakened by my children crying of hunger. My wife tried to feed them some soup but their crying only grew. I sat helplessly before them, covered my face, and began to cry.

"At that moment, I decided to go. If the trucks arrived, I would return with flour; if they didn't, I would at least die on my feet, not sitting watching my children being mauled by hunger.

"When my wife saw me putting on my coat she cried out: 'You know what it means to go out at this hour! The Zionists will bomb you. You will die and leave us alone.'

"Nevertheless, I left. I walked on my way to my death, and at every step I said to myself: *I shall be killed now ... dogs will eat my remains!* I regretted my actions, but my desperation was stronger than my regret.

"I arrived to huge crowds of people, a gathering of the hungry, of skeletons. I saw my friends. The moment I saw them, the trucks began to enter.

"But they did not stop. The drivers were compelled to drive on, as they had been told: if a truck stops, we will bomb it.

"As they entered, people began climbing on the speeding trucks. One young man jumped onto a truck but his leg got caught in the wheel well. The truck ran over him and his leg was crushed up to the knee. He fell beside it, his leg severed, the bones crushed. No one cared. They treaded on his leg as though it was a stepping stone.

"My friends and I managed to climb on top and make it to the front, guarding two sacks of flour. At the rear, a man climbed onto the middle of the truck and started yelling like a madman:

'Finally . . . We'll eat bread!' Then he started throwing sacks onto the ground.

"But with all the pushing, he fell off the truck. His head hit the ground. Last I saw he was squatting on his knees, bleeding like a waterfall from his mouth. Then he fainted. I expect that he died, without eating his first loaf of bread.

"He died shouting with false joy. He died because of hunger.

"As soon as the truck drew near our car, we threw the two sacks of flour to our friends who were waiting for us next to the car. They had managed to get hold of four sacks of flour and half a sack of onions themselves.

"Six bags of flour and half a bag of onions . . . That was all we got out of the battle of flour.

"We gathered near the car with our 'spoils of war.' We were laughing and crying at the same time, laughing because we had survived and crying for the tragic condition into which we had descended.

"Suddenly an armed gang appeared. They weren't just hungry, they were known in the area . . . known to be supported by the occupation. They steal flour to sell on the black market at exorbitant prices. They used to sell a sack weighing twenty-five kilograms for 1,300 US dollars.

"They attacked us violently. They tore one sack of flour and half a sack of onions from the front seat. I jumped into the driver's seat and my friend leapt into the back seat on top of the remaining sacks of flour. I stepped on the gas pedal as hard as I could. The car took off while bullets flew around us.

"One of them suddenly stepped in front of us and fired directly at the windshield. Shattered glass flew into my face like rain, but I did not stop. I drove like death was chasing me until I arrived at Jabalia, where I live.

"And there, the joyful celebrations began.

"Joy mixed with blood and sweat and oppression, joy in bread obtained under fire and bullets. Bread unlike any other bread, bread that was all blood.

"A week later, it was time for the entry of new trucks. The team set off to meet them, but this time we took whatever crude weapons we could find, knives and iron rods, in case the gangs that had robbed us attacked us again.

"We arrived by car at ten o'clock in the evening. We started a fire near the car and sat down around it, same as the last time.

"Suddenly two tanks appeared from the south followed by the trucks. They didn't go far this time, stopping only fifty meters beyond the occupation's checkpoint and unloading their cargo there, a large pile of flour sacks. Then the tanks retreated quietly.

"The place fell silent. We were dumbfounded. *Why? What was going on? Why did they unload the flour like that?* None of us had an answer. We waited for a few minutes, fearful of a trick or a trap.

"Silence among soldiers was unusual, uncharacteristic of them. Still, the flour was there, close by, enticing us.

"We moved slowly at first, then we broke into a run, all of us, like we were in a marathon where the prize was life.

"But as soon as we reached the pile of flour, the firing began.

"The man next to me was clutching his sack like he was holding a baby, running with determination when a sniper's bullet suddenly severed his head entirely. His body continued running for a few moments, his head rolling in front of him until he fell, blood gushing from his neck, pouring onto the sack of flour.

"I was carrying a sack as well. I dropped it and ran like lightning until I reached our car, hiding behind it while the bullets rained down.

"Three young men in front of me were dragging a sack together. The sniper fired his first bullet, hitting one in the leg. He fell to the ground screaming. The second man tried to escape but a bullet ripped through his chest and brought him down. The third froze in place in a panic—a bullet got him in the eye and exited his head, the final punctuation mark of their story."

Abu Malek turned to me. "I don't know what to tell you son . . . I don't know. They are not human, they are monsters."

He continued, "The field was full of body parts. Blood was everywhere. When the rest of my friends joined me, we crawled away towards the north. We crawled, afraid of bullets. Afraid the sniper would see us and repeat his deed.

"We left the car behind and we left our dying brethren. Many were shouting, calling, bleeding, but no one answered. Those who were not killed outright were only steps from death; bleeding, twisting, then falling silent forever.

"My trusted friend told me that a Zionist bulldozer came by after we had withdrawn and dug a very large hole in the sandy beach.

Then collected all the corpses and body parts of the wounded and the martyrs and threw them there. Then they covered them with the rubble."

He sighed and went on: "They are using us to amuse themselves, using us for training. In a single day, 109 people were martyred. After that, the place acquired the name: Dawar Almout, or 'Roundabout of Death.'"[1]

Letting out a laugh dripping with sarcasm and bitterness, he added, "After that, I decided to die from hunger . . . rather than go to the trucks."

He was silent for a moment. "But there is one thing I want to tell you . . . " he said. "The next day I found a sack of flour tied over a cart . . . It was red and it smelled like blood."

Tea was served . . . without sugar.

Even as Abu Salem spoke to me, I could see that signs of famine had begun to appear on his face. This was from the new famine that began with the Zionists' violation of the ceasefire and their return to complete the operation to annihilate us.

After the first sip, he continued: "Now, I use a different method.

---

1 The Nabulsi Roundabout Massacre, also referred to as the "Flour Massacre" (*majzarat at-taḥīn*), stands as one of the most harrowing atrocities of the genocide in Gaza. On February 29, 2024, after enduring months of siege-induced starvation, thousands of starving Palestinians gathered at the Nabulsi Roundabout in Gaza City to receive aid. Trucks carrying sacks of flour—lifesaving food after months of siege and starvation—entered the area. Israeli occupation forces opened fire on the crowd who had assembled to secure food for their families, killing and injuring hundreds in what became a symbol of the weaponization of food, starvation, and collective punishment. The majority of injuries treated were due to gunshot wounds and the victims included children and individuals with catastrophic injuries to the head, neck and chest.

"I returned to Beit Hanoun—our town that was destroyed by the Zionists—with other families. We took up residence in the school at the entrance to the town, and from there our work began.

"The plan was simple . . . I would get in touch with people I knew who had been displaced to the south and ask them about the location of flour and food in their homes. Most of the houses had been demolished . . . actually, almost all of them had.

"One of my relatives told me he had left a full barrel of flour in his kitchen before he left.

"So I went. His house had been bombed, and its ceiling completely caved in. After half an hour of digging through the collapsed roof, my brother and I managed to create a small hole no more than 40 centimeters in diameter.

"I crawled inside. The space was so tight I couldn't lift my head or move my shoulders. Suddenly I found a broken plate. I was delighted. I realized that I was close to the kitchen.

"I took the plate with me. When I reached the kitchen, I found that the ceiling's remains were pressing down on the barrel of flour. I made a hole at the bottom of the barrel and started scooping out the flour onto the plate using a spoon I had found. Then I crawled backwards until I reached my brother who would empty the plate into a sack he had found nearby. The flour had a grey color as it was mixed with gunpowder from the missiles, but it was flour.

"Another time, after many efforts to break through the roof of another house, we found a sack of flour, but it had turned into stone. The rain had soaked it until it hardened, and it was full of insect nests. Nevertheless, we unearthed it like it was treasure.

"We set about breaking it up and then passing it through a sieve until it was usable as flour. In spite of all the hardship and danger and frustration, it was better than Dawar Almout."

He continued: "It went on like that until the ceasefire. Even when the planes began to drop aid packages, I did not go. I had seen enough scenes of suffering, shoving, and sorrow. The only thing that kept me going each day were my children and my mother."

He sighed. "You know, I lost 35 kilograms," he said, hoarse. "Each day half a kilo would melt away, half a kilo of my body, and many times that from my soul."

My friend Mousa

Mousa is my friend, an ambitious, hardworking, cheerful guy who was studying information technology at university.

After the occupation's violation of the ceasefire, we were displaced a second time from Beit Hanoun and my cousin and I met him with a few others in Gaza City. We sat in a corner amidst the rubble and I asked him to describe in detail what they had been through during their steadfastness in the north.

He sighed slightly. "In the name of God . . . Let the horror film begin.

"First, we were forced to eat animal fodder and weeds. We called that month the 'green month' due to the amount of weeds we gathered and ate.

"After that, the trucks began to enter from south to the north. At the beginning they used to take al-Rashid Road. We met them at the Nabulsi Roundabout which came to be known as Dawar Almout.

"The trucks would enter at an insane speed. People set up barriers in their path, but they did not stop, even if the roadblocks were human bodies. If a driver were to stop he would be shelled. The Zionists told them: 'Stopping is prohibited under any circumstances.' They were the ones who created the tragedy with their own hands, and then watched as we devoured each other.

"Hungry people attacked the trucks as they would attack prey. The trucks were full of flour, running like enraged bulls.

"My brother, cousins, and I were the first to jump on the first truck. We began by tearing the plastic off the bags and tossing the coverings aside. Then we climbed up onto the roof of the truck's cabin to secure what bags we could, keeping them out of the crowd's reach until the truck got far enough and we could escape with our haul. We got hold of eight sacks. We sat on top of them, guarding them with our bodies.

"A young man clambered onto the truck behind us and began to climb. When he got to the top he tried to rip off the plastic cover, but because of the crowding and shoving, he fell.

"The cover wrapped around his leg and he got caught in the plastic. His body slid down, his head scraping the ground. But his arm still clutched the sack of flour.

"Do you know what happened next?

"The hungry people ran towards him, not to save him, but to snatch the sack of flour from his hands."

Astonished, I asked, "People from Gaza did that?!"

Mousa covered his face with his hands. "Be quiet, Wasim. Be quiet! Hunger is bad, Wasim. When you have children crying from hunger right in front of you, you will do whatever you can so that they can eat."

"Were you there on the day the Nabulsi Roundabout massacre took place?" I asked. "The massacre in which over one hundred people were killed?"

He sighed. *"Alhamdullilah*, fortunately I didn't go that day. We intended to go, but we could not find fuel for the car."

Then he raised his head, as though he was contemplating something unseen. "Did you know, Wasim? To this day, no one knows the fate of those who went missing there. Days later, some people went back to look for the bodies of their relatives and the remains of their brothers, but they found nothing."

He continued in a hushed voice: "But I was a witness to another massacre. It happened on Salah al-Din Road, near the Kuwait Roundabout, the second road along which the trucks entered shortly after the Nabulsi massacre.

"It was a cold and rainy night, with heavy clouds and aircraft in the sky. The sky lit up, sometimes by lightning and sometimes by missiles. People were waiting for the trucks there, the place known as the Kuwait Roundabout. I remember when it used to be one of the most beautiful and lively areas of Gaza. Now, there are no streets, no roundabout, and no houses. Everything has been bulldozed and destroyed. It is now just an open field, covered with shrapnel and the remnants of houses.

"That night the square was packed with people, as if a famous singer was about to perform. But the difference was that everyone was hungry, thirsty, and terrorized.

"Suddenly they fired smoke bombs at us. We couldn't see anything. Silence fell, the silence of fear. Then we heard the sound of propellers. I raised my eyes and the only thing I could see through the smoke was a quadcopter drone[1] above us. Then it started shooting.

"There wasn't just one, but a large number of drones. They fired randomly. We ran in all directions, not knowing where to go. The smoke obscured the view, and everyone was shoving.

"I fell. My face hit the muddy ground, but I got up and continued running until I reached our car.

"Some of my cousins were there, their limbs trembling, their faces pale. They were asking me: 'Where are they? Your brother? So and so? Have you seen them? May God protect them. They may be dead.'

"Suddenly one of them approached my head and removed something that was dangling from my hair. It was a piece of human flesh. It was someone's throat.

"At that moment I realized that what I thought was mud was nothing but blood and body parts.

"We dug a small hole and buried the throat, and we prayed for mercy for its owner."

Mousa was silent for a moment, then his voice suddenly rose, his hands trembling: "Do you see, Wasim? When a human being in Gaza is killed, cut to bits while hungry, people walk on his body

---

1   The Israeli occupation army uses "quadcopter" drones—originally developed for surveillance and monitoring—as direct killing tools that target Palestinian civilians with explosive bombs and live ammunition, carrying out assassinations in the field from afar. Between February and March 2024, as limited aid convoys entered northern Gaza, the occupation forces used quadcopter drones to shell and open fire at Palestinians waiting for aid at the Kuwait Roundabout and Nabulsi Roundabouts. Along with targeting food distribution sites, these drones have drastically altered the lives of civilians, tracking them through narrow alleys and attacking them inside their shelters and tents, causing waves of terror and destruction.

parts and it's all over. Even his family . . . they won't even find a grave to visit him."

Silence grew between us. Then he sighed: "Let me continue. While we were beside the hole where we buried the young man's throat, we prayed for him and wept, for him and for ourselves. All of a sudden we saw the lights of a truck approaching us. At the rear my brother and another young man were fighting over a sack of flour entangled in the wooden frame of the trailer.

"My brother yelled: 'Mousa! Mousa! Prepare an empty sack. Get ready.'

"I grabbed a sack and ran alongside the truck. I raised it up to my brother, and he pulled out a knife and cut open the entangled sack and began shoveling the flour with his hands into the sack I was carrying. I was faster than the truck that day."

Mousa looked at me. "Do you know, Wasim? After we got back, we found that some of the flour had been mixed with mud and had become dough. Despite this, we began to collect it."

In the middle of that conversation, I asked him about the throat of the young man which they had buried: "What was that young man's fault, brother? What did he do to be killed like that?"

He answered: "It wasn't only one young man, brother—there were many of them. While I was on top of the truck, I saw their body parts. There were a lot of them—the truck ran over their body parts."

He was quiet for a moment, then said: "Wasim, it was flour full of suffering, mud, and body parts."

"Did you try to get hold of aid that was parachuted in?"

He replied, smiling sadly: "Yes—it was surreal. I saw things which I thought only happened in video games: a huge military cargo plane with a gigantic propeller, exactly like those we see in *PUBG: Battlegrounds*. The size of one propeller alone is sufficient to make you stop in awe, its blades stand out like blades of death. It is painted dark black or a military green, and on its tail is the flag of the country that lies to us."

He continued, waving his hand as though he was seeing it anew: "The planes came down low, opened their rear cargo doors, and began discharging parachutes. Each plane discharged twelve parachutes, huge parachutes, each nearly a hundred square meters in area. We later took them and made tents out of them, yes! We would take shelter underneath them. Each parachute carried a wooden box, one cubic meter in size and weighing about a ton, which was dropped from the sky about one kilometer away, most often along the seacoast. And on the sandy beach, hundreds of hungry people were running in every direction. The wind was the only thing determining the direction in which people ran, wind that toyed with the parachutes and our hearts."

He paused for a few seconds. "We used to wait for them as though we were a wilting plant waiting for rain. We were lifeless bodies waiting for our souls to descend from the sky.

"When the prized 'treasures' reached the ground, the hungry pounced on them, hundreds of people on top of one another, a violent struggle and fierce stampede, fighting over a can of fava beans or a handful of rice."

Mousa lifted his hat, pointing to a scar on his forehead, and added: "This wound was from my first day there. After people attacked the first box, the plane dropped a second one near us. I left the crowd and ran as hard as I could towards it. I was not running after it, I was racing towards it to catch it, my heart racing joyfully ahead of me. Suddenly, I found myself stretched out on the ground, being carried by my brother and cousins, bleeding from my face. They told me that the bottom of the wooden box hit my head and knocked me out."

My cousin interjected: "Had the wind not been strong, it would have fallen on top of you and crushed you."

"Due to my injury, we were only able to get two cans of fava beans and a kilo of dates."

A third friend who was sitting with us interrupted to say: "In Deir al-Balah, they dropped parachutes on us only once, but the only beneficiaries were the fish in the sea. The parachutes came down one kilometer offshore!"

He turned to Mousa: "I saw pictures of parachutes that fell without opening—they crushed the people underneath them. They say this was filmed in northern Gaza. Were you there?"

Mousa replied: "*Alhamdullilah*, I wasn't there. That was in the first week after my injury and I did not leave where I was staying because of that. However, my cousin was there. He saw with his own eyes the bodies that were crushed under that cursed box. He saw blood coming out of their eyes, their ears, their noses. Their bodies exploded from the inside, Wasim!"

He paused again and then resumed: "As for the sea, the same thing happened to us as it did to you. Everything fell into the water. That was on the first or second day I went out after my injury, I can't recall exactly. We set off at six in the morning, we reached the beach at seven and waited for the planes which usually came at nine."

He sighed. "The planes came, they descended, the door opened, the parachutes dropped, cries of joy emanated from the hungry as they raised their heads towards the sky, their eyes shining from tears and the sun.

"But suddenly, the parachutes began to drift towards the sea. They all fell very far from the beach. Cries of desperation and frustration rang out. We lowered our heads, the glint in our eyes, extinguished. Those who knew how to swim began to do so, and those who could not swim . . . the faces of their hungry children swam in their imagination. "

His voice broke as he said: "I swam alone, reached one of the boxes, tore the plastic off the top packages. I took one in my arms, tore off a thin board of wood, put two additional packages on it and began to paddle back with all three to the shore.

"On the way back I saw a child drowning. I called out to him: 'Can you swim? Go back! You will drown!'

'Save me, help me!' he screamed. 'I can't do it!'

"I drew close to him, made him grasp the piece of wood. I yelled: 'You were about to die. Why'd you do this?'

'My father was martyred,' he said, crying. 'I am the oldest among my brothers. We don't have any food.'

"I replied, hoarse: 'Don't be afraid. You will get your share of what I got.'

"We reached the shore. My brother and cousins were there to meet me. As I opened the package, I gave a share to the child."

Mousa stopped suddenly and said: "Down the way, on another stretch of the beach people gathered and began to yell. There was no box there. There was a deaf child . . . hungry . . . who had drowned and died!

"The child I had saved embraced me with all his strength and said, crying: '*Shukran Yabba*, thank you Dad, thank you.'" Mousa was silent for a long time, and then ended his testimony in a faltering voice: "That is our story, Wasim; the birds of paradise turned out to be the dragons of evil. It was all a ploy, criminal media propaganda, a new kind of torture and humiliation for us."

Anonymous man in the market

One day, I was buying from a merchant who was offering rotten flour, reeking of a foul smell. He was selling it for forty shekels per kilogram, the equivalent of ten dollars. I asked him for three kilograms, but when I was about to pay him, I burst out angrily: "What injustice! Rotten flour at this price? What sort of life is this?!"

Suddenly, a young man put his hand on my shoulder and said: "It is good that there is flour!" Then he held his leg, amputated above the knee, and shook it with sorrow and bitterness, before adding: "See?! For flour, I lost my leg . . . and I lost fifteen family members . . . that was the price we paid for that damned flour, which we never even got."

A moment of heavy silence fell on the narrow store. I took my flour without a word and left, and I waited for him outside the door. When he came out, I greeted him and told him that I was writing a book on Gaza, about our pain, so that the entire world would hear our voice. I asked him to tell me his story.

He was silent for a minute, then he balanced himself on his crutches and leaned his back against the wall. "Write to them," he said. "Write that there is a young man from Gaza who was sitting with his friends and relatives. Our children around us were crying from hunger. Then, suddenly we heard the news: the flour trucks had arrived!

"We rushed immediately to al-Rashid Road. On the way our only conversations were:

'Finally, we'll be done with that cursed green soup!

'We won't eat animal feed any more!

'We'll become human again!

'We'll feed our children . . . ' All we hoped for was just a bite to silence their hunger. We weren't asking for more.

"We arrived and waited a bit until the trucks arrived. They unloaded their cargo near the checkpoint. Strangely, there were no soldiers there. Just flour! We ran towards it . . .

"Then, I don't know what happened. I woke up in a pile of body parts. I saw my relatives' heads, their brains scattered on the sidewalk . . . Their intestines, their feet . . . Even my foot was there, severed. Blood was flowing from my leg like a waterfall.

"I took off my shirt and tied it around my leg, but the blood did not stop. My stomach was ripped open. I began to crawl, until a young man came and saved my life."

The youth fell silent. He cried and muttered: "Pray for God's mercy on them . . . Pray that they will be compensated for the hell that they have lived through."

A moment later he spoke again, defeated: "Young man, if the blood of those I love have not aroused the sympathy of the world yet, do you think that your words will?"

I shook my head, certain that he was right. I repeated to myself: *If a year and seven months of bloodshed hasn't moved anyone . . . will ink on paper?*

"I'll go now," he continued. "The kids went to sleep hungry yesterday, I want to feed them today."

In truth, my search for testimonies about hunger wasn't difficult. Every individual in Gaza is a witness and has a story to tell. Every person in Gaza can write volumes about incidents of suffering and sorrow if asked.

Yet with every witness account I have heard, I felt there were those who couldn't tell theirs . . . whose voices ended before they began. This opened another door for me: to recount the testimonies of those who could not say anything, whose voices we will not hear, whose faces we will not see. I shall try to narrate the cases of those who have been annihilated, who disappeared from this world, the only mention of them being a small item at the end of a news bulletin: "A number of people were martyred."

But does anyone know how they were killed? What was their crime? How did those monsters take pleasure in wiping them out?

Many pictures and videos have emerged, making their way to this living world that has seen what we have lived through. However, no one has been moved. It was no more than a momentary trend, a hobby that helped pass the time. And behold, the genocide is getting more intense from day to day. Each moment is worse than the one before.

This is why I decided to write how my loved ones have been killed, how my people were exterminated. I write only in the hope that this pain will stir something in the future generations.

In fact, given the hardships I'm living through, I am absolutely sure that no one will hear my voice. I am certain that they will kill me as they have done to sixty thousand of my people. And they continue . . .

I hope that the ink I am writing with will stem the continuous hemorrhage, this endless bleeding that will only stop when the blood of the last Palestinian on this earth has been spilled.

If global action is not taken, we will be wiped out. We shall become a story, a fairy tale, a memory on the margins of history.

Untold Tragedies . . .
Martyrs without Witnesses[1]

---

1   In Arabic, the word *shaheed* can mean either martyr or witness, as both terms share an etymological root and are linguistically related.

Massacre around
the Indonesian Hospital

During the first storming of the area around the Indonesian Hospital,[1] they imposed a strict siege on the neighborhood and a curfew on the surrounding schools.

A child was playing in front of the door of his classroom when a treacherous sniper's bullet pierced his chest.

What was his crime? That he tried to steal a moment of fun from the jaws of terror.

What was his sin? That he tried to laugh, to forget, even for a moment, that he was in the presence of monsters.

A bullet killed him.[2] It killed his playtime, and his mother's heart too.

---

1   The Indonesian Hospital is located in the Jabalia refugee camp, and was the first hospital built in Gaza since the Zionist siege and blockade began in 2006. The occupation forces laid siege to the Indonesian Hospital in November 2023 during which they perpetrated several massacres, including targeting the surrounding area with fire belts and besieging the hospital with snipers who executed anyone who moved inside, including medical staff and wounded patients.

2   The Israeli journalist Nati Yefet reported details of an encounter he had with a former Israeli soldier. The soldier was suffering from a serious head wound, and it turned out that the injury was the result of fighting in Gaza. During the conversation, Yefet asked the soldier if he was receiving proper treatment, to which he replied: "Excellent treatment, physically and psychologically." After a moment of

They carried the small, blood-soaked body inside the classroom, under the cover of silence.

Bitter hours passed.

Everyone began to exchange their memories of him, whispering his name, recalling his laughter . . . he was amongst them, but he was not with them.

He was there in a body without a spirit, a mere shadow of a childhood cut short.

His grandfather, grandmother, father, and uncles decided to bury him, hoping that it would ease his mother's suffering and honor the innocent body of their angel.

They went out.

His grandfather carried him in his hands, hands cracked with age and sorrow, while his father, uncles, and grandmother raised white flags with hands that were trembling with sorrow and fear. They buried him next to the school.

On their way back, as soon as they drew near the school gate, two accursed bullets hit the father and the grandfather in the head. Their brains scattered on the sidewalk.

---

silence, the soldier continued: "I will never be okay. Don't you get it? I was a sniper in Gaza. After I had killed two hundred people I stopped counting."

The journalist was shocked and asked the soldier if there were many like him. He answered confidently: "Of course. I know a person from a *moshav*, a form of Zionist agriculture settlement, near Sderot who stopped counting after four hundred."

When asked if the dead included children, he answered: "Not in my case, but generally, yes." A moment later he sighed and said in a faint voice: "Yes, there were children . . . There were children."

The others tried to carry their bodies, but the bullets would not stop. They sheltered behind their loved ones, hid under them, and raised those white flags again, the flags of surrender.

But monsters do not recognize flags or surrender, they only recognize death and blood.

Their wives and children were standing at the door to the classroom, screaming, crying, imploring.

But no one could do anything.

Minutes later, two more bullets hit the two uncles in the head. They fell, as did their flags, and their white flags soon turned red.

Then a final bullet hit the grandmother, heartbroken and devastated over the loss of her children, in the head. A cursed bullet that silenced her last calls for help.

Two days passed, and the school became a prison of silence and terror.

Two days while bodies lay stretched out on the ground, women stared at the corpses of their husbands in impotent silence, children stared at their fathers while cats ate their scattered brains on the sidewalk and the dogs tore at their flesh.

Are you waiting for me to tell you that they were buried two days later?

No!

Instead the monsters came and arrested the remaining men and expelled the women and children.

The wives begged the monsters, pleading with the soldiers for permission to say farewell, to kiss the foreheads of their loved ones. But the monsters refused, threatening that they would meet the same fate as the men.

People returned to the area a month and a half later to find a hole in the school containing the family's five bodies . . . bodies that had been mangled by the dogs and the monsters.

Next to them were twenty white body bags, each containing a body with its hands tied, and in each forehead a sniper's bullet.

In Gaza, white no longer means peace. It has become the color of death.

They burned inside the classroom

It was a rainy and terrifying night.

At 1:30 a.m. the monsters had infiltrated further. The sound of their tank treads tore apart the stillness. Darkness gave way to a day lit not by light from the sky, but by flames from hell.

Shells rained down, aircraft dropping cursed cluster bombs made in the land of "freedom and democracy" as their citizens call it.

People had been displaced from the regions around Abraj al-Nada, fleeing death for what they thought would be life. Among them were the brothers Ahmad and Ali and their families: Ahmad with his wife and three children and Ali with his wife and five children.

This was their sixth displacement.

They left barefoot, hungry, terrified, carrying nothing with them . . . Only fear and pain.

They followed a muddy road, wet from rain and death, for two kilometers until they reached the school where their father and third brother lived. There, the tears of those fleeing death mixed with the tears of those waiting for it. They hugged each other with arms shaking from the cold and the terror.

They went up to a classroom on the third floor. Step by step, they were lulled into a sense of safety; they reached the room, believing it would be their refuge, their "paradise."

Everyone went to sleep, their bodies wet from the rain, their feet caked with mud, their eyes exhausted from late nights and terror. They fell asleep, thinking they had survived.

But death was lurking from behind the window.

Suddenly, a shell fell. It did not wake them up; it tore them to pieces. Its flames penetrated the walls, and the shrapnel shredded their bodies.

Five of them were blown out of the classroom's iron windows, past the school campus: their mother, one of the brother's wives, and three children. Their bodies flew, their souls fell.

As for the rest?

The classroom caught fire. Fire surrounded them, burning their thin, cold, and hungry bodies. Their limbs were torn by the flying debris and what remained of their bodies were devoured by the flames before their liquefying eyes.

Blood boiled, wounds bled, and faces melted.

The women clutched the iron bars on the windows with melting fingers, screaming—but the fire melted their screams too.

Their children were running, deformed, screaming without sound, melting like candles in hellfire.

Residents of the school tried to put out the fire but were unable to.

Suddenly, more shells landed on the school, on the shelter, on the survivors.

Many were killed and wounded. The rest fled.

They ran carrying their mother, "the mother of the burning ones," her bones shattered, her hip broken, her gaze frozen on the classroom that had devoured her family. She was screaming, crying, calling her children, hearing their screams as they burned and burning with them.

People returned to the area three days later, and the fire was out.

But it was all over. It was over for everyone in the classroom.

There was nothing left but ashes, the ashes of the furniture, and the ashes of their bones.

Fifteen martyrs, whose skulls and the collected remains of their burned bones, were placed in a single shroud . . .

The dog took a bite out of the face of the newborn

She was pregnant. She lived in a classroom, in a school where thousands of people sought refuge after shelling engulfed their homes.

On a rainy night, she was caught off guard by labor pains.

The only people around were her neighbor and her little ten-year-old daughter. And her husband? Missing for weeks. She did not know if he was alive or if he had been turned to ashes under the rubble of the collapsed houses.

So she went to the hospital without her family; just her neighbor and the fetus struggling to survive amidst the screams of his mother and the missiles, in the darkness of the womb and the darkness of bitter reality.

No one helped her. There was no hand to rest on her back, no watchful eye to reassure her heart. She gave birth to a baby boy whom she named after his missing father. It was as if the name was a lifeline, as though she was trying to resurrect her husband from the jaws of death. She held the baby to her chest.

With no tears left to shed, she hid a small piece of paper under his clothes, on which she wrote in trembling handwriting: the name of the child, his father's name, and the name of the school where she was living.

The doctors were asking mothers to do this because death was closer than breast feeding.

After midnight, she tried to return by ambulance with her neighbor and newborn baby. The road to the school was flooded with water, silence, and terror.

However, the shell was not far away. Suddenly, it struck.

The ambulance caught fire, swallowed up by the inferno. The bodies scattered, and the screams were consumed by the flames.

No one came. The bodies remained on the street, under the rain, until dawn.

The following day, an ambulance came and collected the corpses and body parts from the road and from the burnt ambulance: black bones, flesh turned into coal, and a silent scream which remained suspended above the broken glass.

Hours later, three young men were passing near a stretch of land covered with thorns by the side of the road. They heard moaning, and when they approached they found him! The newborn!

Lying among the thorns, his face was covered in dirt and the side of his cheek was bleeding.

It was a dog's bite.

But the baby was alive, as though his mother's corpse, even though it was torn apart, still embraced him, keeping away the flames, the dogs, and death. It was as though she had told the world: "Eat me . . . but leave him alone."

She had turned her corpse into a shield, her death gave him life.

They lifted the torn cloth on his chest and found the piece of paper stuck to his tiny body underneath, wet with his blood— the blood that had flowed from his bitten cheek.

But the name . . . It had not been erased.

His mother had written it and hidden it upon his chest, as though she knew that her body would be forgotten but she did not want him to be forgotten.

They took him back to the school. His ten-year-old sister hugged him as though she was embracing her mother, her father, and all that was left of the family.

She raised him out of fear, not out of experience.

She nursed him with her pain, not with milk.

She sang to him in a broken voice and tended to his open wound.

And as for the scar on his cheek?

It remains there.

An eternal mark that says: "I was killed . . . before I was born."

'Yamma,
I don't want to die.'

At the entrance of Beit Hanoun, there was a school where people thought they had found refuge.

Suddenly, without warning, shells began to rain down randomly everywhere.

The tanks drew near; the sound of their caterpillar treads grew louder as the earth itself cried out from beneath their metal tracks.

A projectile burst through the door of one of the classrooms, a room where a trembling family had taken refuge: a mother, her oldest son (a young man in his twenties), two daughters, and a small child. A month earlier, their father had been taken prisoner by the monsters, the same day they were displaced from the last school they had been sheltering at.

The shell's shrapnel cut off the oldest son's leg above the knee. There was profuse bleeding, an endless stream of blood. They tried to stem the bleeding with everything they had, but the only thing they found was a rusty iron wire which they tied around his leg in the hope that it would stop the flow of blood. They loaded him on a donkey cart and rushed him to the Indonesian Hospital three kilometers away.

As soon as they reached the main street, quadcopter drones began to fire bullets and bombs around them, chasing them as though they were prey in the desert.

The donkey was killed!

The grieving mother and the driver of the cart carried the son and took cover behind the rubble of a house, until could return to the school on foot. With each step they left a trail of the young man's blood.

They arrived back at their classroom. The mother cradled him in her lap, as she used to do when he was sick as a child; except this time the disease was not a passing one.

His hand was cold, his lips had turned blue, and his eyes were quivering.

He said in a broken voice: "*Yamma*, oh mom, I don't want to die!"

She did not reply. She couldn't. All she saw was the open wound in his leg and the unstoppable stream of blood. She placed her hand on his chest. She could feel his pulse weakening, second by second.

"*Yamma*, I'm cold . . . "

She covered him with her abaya, with her tears, with her trembling words: "Please God, please let my son live!"

His eyes opened for the last time, giving her a look of apology, resignation, farewell.

Then they closed.

His body sagged in her lap, and everything stopped.

Time stood still.

She continued to cradle him, gently shaking him, as though to awaken him from a nightmare. She refused to believe it: "Don't die . . . Don't leave me . . . You are all that I have left . . ."

But he died.

He died, leaving blood in her lap that could not be washed away, and pain that could not be forgotten.

She kept staring at his severed leg, at his lifeless face, at his sisters' tears, and at their sense of helplessness as they thought of their father, the prisoner.

The son passed away . . . He passed away.

They placed their mother's body in the refrigerator

A displaced family took refuge in a large house next to a school in Gaza City. It was a spacious house, with walls still standing, a roof that still kept off the rain, and a small garden where life still grew despite everything. They thought fortune had finally smiled on them.

The house was deserted. Its owner was rich and absent.

As the father inspected the place, he said: "We shall live here in safety. This is where we'll start over."

On a morning that was calmer than usual, the mother started a small fire in the garden, planning to cook some lentils. She put the pot on top of the stones and sat on the ground, her six-month-old baby sleeping on her lap, breathing softly.

Life, in all its details, was there: smoke rising softly, sunlight filtering through the branches of olive trees, and the laughter of children drifting out of the windows.

Then . . . the shot was fired.

One shot—silent, precise, sudden—fired from a distance, by an eye that only saw a moving target.

It pierced her chest, and everything stopped.

The mother fell on the ground, the baby on top of her. The blood flowed swiftly, as though her heart was bleeding everything that she had been unable to say throughout the months of war.

Her husband ran to her, picked her up in his arms, yelling: "We need a hospital. Someone help us! We need a hospital!"

But he could not find a way.

The sniper was there, observing, hunting, preventing even the air from moving.

They tried opening the door . . . Bullets.

They tried going out the rear window. . . Bullets.

They failed. They remained prisoners of the house. Death was at every corner. The mother bled for long hours. She bled till she was dry.

Then she was still.

She died.

The baby that was lying in her lap, cried nonstop.

They wanted to bury her.

They tried digging a hole in the garden of the house. But the bullets were flying over their heads, giving an explicit warning: "You have no rights, even over your deaths."

In a corner of the kitchen there was a solar-powered refrigerator.

They looked at it—silence overwhelmed them.

The refrigerator was vertical, tall, and not suitable for such a thing. But they had no other choice.

They tried laying the refrigerator on the ground, horizontally, so that her children could see her one last time, to say goodbye. But they couldn't do it. It was made of heavy iron, its door would not open easily, and the space was narrow.

Following several painful efforts, they lifted her body . . . They wrapped her in black plastic bags, tied her with ropes so that she would not fall, then they opened the refrigerator door with difficulty. They put her in, upright.

Yes, they put their mother in the refrigerator, standing up.

There was no coffin in the house, so the refrigerator became her coffin.

There was no grave in the neighborhood, so the kitchen became her grave.

Days passed.

On the first day, one of her children came up to the refrigerator, opened the door a crack. "*Yamma*," they whispered, their voice breaking, "why don't you speak?"

During the days that followed they sat around her. They told her about a day that did not start, about a breakfast that was not cooked, about games that were not played. They spoke of hunger, of fear, and of her voice that used to fill the place . . .

But she did not answer.

They knew they were alone, but they were waiting for her to wake up . . . Just to wake up.

After ten full days, the sound of gunfire grew fainter.

The father summoned all his strength and opened the refrigerator.

Her body had changed.

She was entirely blue.

Her features were frozen, her hands had hardened, as though death had stiffened her so that she would remain fixed in her children's memories forever. She no longer resembled herself, but she was still their mother.

They wrapped her in a light blanket, and the father carried her out at the first crack of dawn. He did not get very far.

A nearby cemetery? There was none.

But the grounds of al-Shifa Hospital weren't far away.

There, among the crumbling walls, under a sky smothered with smoke, they dug a small grave for her and buried her quietly.

Then the children went back to the house. To the garden where she had been cooking ten days earlier. But the place had changed.

It had become cold.

As cold as the refrigerator that had contained her body.

As cold as the heart of her child which had tasted sorrow before tasting childhood.

They were crushed alive under the treads of a tank

After the monsters invaded one of the shelters in Gaza City, they took all the men prisoner, as they typically did in every invasion. After a full day of torment, torture, and hell, as the commander of the unit which surrounded the school shouted: "People of Gaza, welcome to hell!"

They released some of the men, only nine out of about a hundred men. They released them naked, broken, and humiliated, wearing only their underwear.

One of them later spoke to me. "They had a camp in the area," he said in a voice, faint as though his own breath was stifled. "and we were detained there. After a full day of torture, they decided to release us, but at the gate to the camp, they stopped us and said: 'The tank will show you the path to safety. Start running. If anyone looks back, he is sentencing himself to death.'

"One of them fired a burst of bullets between our feet. We understood it to be the signal to start. We began to run . . . our naked, exhausted, hungry bodies, trembling from fatigue and terror.

"The bullets did not stop. They traced our steps, sometimes getting ahead of us, sometimes running alongside us, sometimes hitting us.

"A few minutes later, we heard one of them yell on the loudspeaker: 'You! Human beasts. Stop!'"

He was silent for a moment, then he cried out bitterly: "They all have the same mentality. The only thing they want is to annihilate us . . . They don't see us as human beings. We knew that he was talking about us. We were the 'human beasts.' We realized that with broken hearts and with our dignity buried underfoot.

"We stopped. Their dogs came, surrounded us, and started barking and howling. They scared us. There were only nine of us in the middle, and bullets were still flying over our heads and under our feet.

"Then the tank started to move . . . a terrifying, heavy, and grotesque death machine. It approached us and a soldier emerged from within the hatch and yelled: 'You dogs! No, you are less than dogs! You insects!' He went on to curse our mothers and our wives, he insulted our dignity, debasing all of humanity with his words. Then he said, 'I'll show you the way . . . I will lead you to the escape route, although you do not deserve it. Start marching. I will be behind you showing you where to go.'

"Then he disappeared into his tank, and we started to scramble in front of it. Humiliation, humiliation, humiliation.

The man speaking to me stifled a sob. He went on:

"Suddenly, the tank picked up speed. It surged towards us and ran over four of us. It crushed them, going forward and reversing, again and again. We ran, with bullets chasing us."

He was quiet, then he cried out, his hand shaking: "I wish they had killed them from the beginning! I wish they had killed them before terrorizing them, before they starved them, before they crushed their dignity and humanity. I wish they had killed them, they crushed them . . .

"I wish they had killed me, from the beginning, before I saw them crushed."

His voice hoarse from crying and shouting, he went on: "After half an hour of running, we reached a shelter. The people there gave us clothes to cover our nakedness, food to silence our hunger, and water to satisfy our thirst. I found an ambulance there. I told the paramedics what I had witnessed . . . about the four who had been crushed."

"A month later I happened upon one of the paramedics whom I had told the story to. I asked him: 'Did you find them?'

"He said: 'Yes, we found them. Only they weren't bodies; rather, they were crushed body parts, flesh that had stuck to the asphalt. They had become shadows on the pavement. We gathered what broken bones we could find, their crushed limbs, and some flesh we were barely able to separate from the ground.'

"Such is our life in Gaza, Wasim. Their leader was not lying when he said: 'People of Gaza, welcome to hell!'

"That is the story of 'the escape route' that we were forced to march. You know what? I think the world believed them when they described us as 'human beasts.'

"Even now we are dying on screens, and no answer."

The first-born son was martyred and the unborn baby miscarried

It was six o'clock in the morning. The father went out to fetch water from a well that was half a kilometer from the school which had become a shelter for them.

Two hours went by and everyone began to panic.

The eldest son went out to look for his father, wondering in his heart: Is he still alive? Or was he martyred before us?

When the son returned, before he reached the door to the school, his mother, who was pregnant, saw him from a classroom window on the second floor.

"What happened to you?" she called to him. "Where's your father?"

But he did not reply.

A treacherous bullet tore through his chest.

That shot rang the alarm for a tragedy that had only just begun. Shells rained down and the sound of bullets drowned out people's labored breathing.

His mother screamed.

She ran, leapt down the stairs, and rushed towards her son. The men at the school tried to hold her back. A tank was at the end of the street, the barrel of its cannon pointing in her son's direction.

She would not be held back.

No one can stop a mother rushing to the aid of her son.

She got hold of his grandfather's wheelchair. He had passed away a few days before. When she got to him, she lifted up her son, put him in the wheelchair, and took off running towards al-Shifa Hospital.

His heart was beating, but it was bleeding more than it was beating.

Trying to breathe, he told her: "Forgive me, *yamma*, I'm dying."

"No, you won't die!" she cried out. "No one's going to die!"

She reached the hospital. The paramedics took him away.

A few minutes later, one of them came back to say: "Your son has been martyred . . . Is there someone to bury him, or should we do it?"

She fell to the ground. Her only son died, after years of raising him, of fear and survival. And she miscarried her unborn child, in her womb, after years of waiting and hoping.

The flour groom

There was a school at the entrance to Beit Hanoun. Inhabited by a few families, the most recent being a young man who had gotten married—half-heartedly—despite the war. He was supposed to have had a honeymoon, but he spent it living between crumbled walls trying to protect his elderly parents and his new wife from hunger.

Days went by and the famine intensified. Everything ran out. They had nothing left to eat.

He had nothing to silence their hunger.

He decided to go out with a bunch of young men, one of whom had a horse-drawn cart. They planned to enter the heart of the city and search under the rubble of houses for anything: flour, rice, even burnt lentils.

He told the others jokingly, with a laugh tinged with hunger and fear: "Let's promise; if one of us is bombed, the rest of us must return his body to his family so that they can say their goodbyes and bury him. Don't steal food from me and leave me to the dogs!"

They all laughed. They did it to calm their fears.

They came to one of the houses and began digging through the collapsed roof. Under the rubble, they found an entire sack of flour! They rejoiced as though they had discovered a treasure in the heart of the desert. They continued digging, searching for more.

But death was faster.

A damned missile.

A single blow.

Their bodies were torn apart . . . The flour was mixed with flesh and bone and blood.

The sole survivor collected their body parts as they were, loaded them on the cart, and returned with them.

At the door of the school, the young groom's father was waiting. He saw his son—or what was left of him—the head barely clinging to the upper torso, no arms at all.

The father grabbed the head, shook it, and screamed at it: "I told you we would rather die of hunger, than you die from a bomb . . . why did you do this to us?"

His wife did not cry.

She sat silently and took hold of his amputated hand, passing her fingers over the wedding ring which had only been worn for a month . . . It was as though she was reassuring herself that love was still there, even if the body was absent.

She bent down over his hand, trembling, kissed it and then whispered: "We did not get to spend our lives together, but I am still committed to my vow."

My Psychological Torment:
Between Ruins and Imagination

The genocide didn't merely destroy my life or everything I owned;
it went far beyond that.
It destroyed me from within.

It blew the calm from my heart,
shattered the stability of my mind,
and infected me with a strange psychological syndrome.

I believe it haunts every soul in Gaza
and nowhere else in the world.

I haven't found a name for it, nor a reference.
I cannot name it
but I can tell you how I live it.

The first time it took hold of me,
I was sitting in our tent,
trying to solve an equation in electromagnetic physics.

Suddenly . . . I went still.

My mind stopped thinking.
I began to *see* my own shattered brain in front of me,
my crushed skull scattered across my books,
blood pooling all around me.

I froze in place.

The sound of gunfire from their warships snapped me back.

I dove to the ground,
hands over my head,
terrified that what I had just imagined
was now becoming my fate.

Seconds later, I imagined a bullet piercing my forehead,
blood drowning my face.

That nightmare was interrupted
by my mother's voice screaming:
"Let's go! They're shooting at the tents!"

Two young women were injured in the tent nearby.

I fled with my mother.
With every step,
I saw my own head rolling ahead of me,
my hands severed,
my feet torn apart . . .
My mother's head, her limbs . . .

From that moment on,
those visions have never left me.

I walk the street
a car passes by
for a moment, I imagine it's been bombed,
its shrapnel splitting me in two.

At the bakery door,
I suddenly see thousands of dismembered bodies around me,
their blood soaking the bread.

One day I was waiting for a friend.
I saw him coming from afar,
we started to smile

Suddenly, I started crying.

I saw him being bombed,
his body parts exploding in my face.

He hugged me and asked:
"What's wrong? Why are you crying?"

I didn't know what to say.

At the queue for water,
I saw the faucet pour blood instead of water.

The bucket in my hand
was filled, torn intestines floating inside.

But the hardest day of all,
was when we were having lunch as a family:
bread, lentils, a bit of arugula.

Suddenly . . .
I saw my mother beside me, headless,
blood pouring from her neck down her body.

I saw my entire family turn to limbs and flesh.

That damned food was mixed with them:
my father's hand in the pot,
my little sister's leg on the bread,
the brains of the rest, shredded
with cats devouring them.

I don't know anymore . . .

I want to cry.

And now I see them again
as I write this book.

With every word I write,
These visions chase me.

The monsters were not content with destroying our home,
bulldozing our land,
killing my future and my dreams . . .

They weren't content with killing the ones I love.

They destroyed me from the inside.

They turned me into a body waiting for death,
with a mind that dies a thousand times every second.

I wasn't among the dead to rest in peace.

They left me alive
but they killed me from within.

I don't know . . .
If I'm conscious,
then I am living through a genocide and famine
unseen in human history.

If my psychological state takes over,
then I live among corpses, blood, and terror.

If I try to sleep,
my nightmares hunt me . . .
the ghosts of my loved ones knock on the doors of my soul.

At night, I no longer know:
Am I awake?
Am I asleep?
Am I trapped in my mind?

Because the three . . .
are all the same.

They contain nothing
but me, the remains, and death.

This is all I could write . . .
The rest is being written now . . . in blood.

If I stay alive, I will finish the story . . .